Editors' Preface to Macmillan *Studies in Economics*

The rapid growth of academic literature in the field of economics has posed serious problems for both students and teachers of the subject. The latter find it difficult to keep pace with more than few areas of the subject so that an inevitable trend towards specialism emerges. The student quickly loses perspective as the maze of theories and models grows, particularly at a time when so much reappraisal of the established paradigms is taking place.

The aim of the 'Macmillan Studies in Economics' is to offer students, and perhaps some teachers as well, short, reasonably critical overviews of developments in selected areas of economics, particularly those in which current controversies are to be found. As far as possible the titles have been selected to form an integrated whole, although inevitably whole areas have been neglected as being unsuited to the style, format and length of the titles in the series.

In some cases the volumes are rather more like essays than surveys. In most cases, however, the aim is to survey the salient literature in a critical fashion. The level of understanding required to read the volumes varies with the complexity of the subject, but they have been generally written to suit the second- and third-year undergraduate seeking to place his reading of the detailed literature in an over-all context. They are *not* textbooks. Instead they seek to give the kind of perspective that might well be lost by reading longer textbooks on their own, or by reading articles in journals. In particular, they should be most suited to pre-examination revision periods. They are not intended to substitute for the essential reading and assimilation of the original works that they seek to survey and assess.

MACMILLAN STUDIES IN ECONOMICS

General Editors: D. C. ROWAN and G. R. FISHER

Executive Editor: D. W. PEARCE

Relative Income Shares

JOHN KING
and
PHILIP REGAN

Lecturers in Economics at the University of Lancaster

© John King and Philip Regan 1976

First published 1976 by
THE MACMILLAN PRESS LTD
London and Basingstoke
Associated companies in New York Dublin
Melbourne Johannesburg and Madras

SBN 333 18454 8

Printed in Great Britain by
THE ANCHOR PRESS LTD
Tiptree, Essex

Contents

Acknowledgements

We are grateful to Alan Airth, Ron Akehurst, Mike Howard and Rod Whittaker for very helpful criticism, and to Shaie Selzer of Macmillan for great patience. All remaining errors and omissions are the responsibility of the authors, whose relative shares in guilt are indeterminate but definitely exhaust the total.

University of Lancaster

John King
Philip Regan

Introduction

Our concern in this book is with the distribution of income between labour and property.[1] Other classifications are possible. In neo-classical theory, for example, income is distributed among the 'factors of production', while for Marxians (and also for neo-Keynesians) the crucial distinction is that between workers and capitalists. Our categories of employment and property income do not exactly correspond either to neo-classical 'factor shares' nor to Marxian 'class shares', although they are considerably closer to the latter. This introductory chapter is devoted to a discussion of some important conceptual problems.

One difficulty is that neither employment nor property income represents a homogeneous category. It is customary to distinguish *wages* and *salaries* as the component parts of employment income, reflecting respectively the pay of manual and non-manual workers. Sometimes this occupational distinction is given an economic interpretation, according to which wages form part of the firm's variable costs, and salaries part of its fixed costs (see our discussion of Kalecki, p. 54 below). Property income is commonly divided into *rent, interest* and *profit* components, which are in turn viewed by neo-classical economists as the returns to three distinct 'factors of production', i.e. 'land', 'capital' and 'entrepreneurship'. There is, finally, the increasingly popular view that a substantial proportion of labour income is in fact property income, resulting from workers' acquisition of 'human capital' through education and training.

The distinction between wages and salaries is of relatively little, and declining, significance. The average wage in 1961

[1] We ignore the 'secondary' distribution of income, via transfer payments, to those who (like pensioners) may neither work nor own property.

was about three-quarters of the average salary, compared with one-third in 1911 ([2] p. 120), and a substantial minority of manual workers earn *more* than the average salary-earner. The gap in social status and economic security has also narrowed appreciably. It is true that the highest salaries are very much higher than the highest wages, and probably reflect control over (if not actual ownership of) property as much as the performance of work; but in quantitative terms they are not particularly important.[1] Nor is it now valid – if it ever was – to treat the distinction between wages and salaries as identical with that between variable and fixed labour costs. Oi [70] has shown that the fixed costs of employment of manual workers are so considerable that wage-earners are better described as constituting a 'quasi-fixed factor of production'.

The neo-classical division of property income into rent, interest and profits is equally problematical. In the first place, the data bear little relationship to the theoretical categories. Secondly, and more important, the categories themselves are open to criticism. Economic rent, for example, is in principle the return to any input over and above its 'transfer earnings', and is thus applicable to all inputs and largely immeasurable. Neo-classical economists themselves are not agreed whether 'entrepreneurship' is or is not a fourth 'factor of production', or whether profits – as opposed to rent and interest – represent the return to such a 'factor', or simply the difference between total and contractual property incomes which arises in an uncertain world. (The best discussion of this whole tortuous debate is [6] ch. 2.) The position is not simplified by the tendency for empirical studies in the neo-classical tradition to rest on the implicit assumption of perfect certainty.

The very concept of 'factors of production' is misleading. It implies that the *natural* characteristics of material objects, rather than the *social* relations of production, determine the way in which income is distributed, so that 'it becomes a property of money to generate value and yield interest, much as it is an attribute of pear trees to bear pears' ([63] p. 392). In fact

---

[1] Although the proliferation of non-cash payments, fringe benefits and 'perks' of various kinds, concentrated among high salary-earners [94], is very difficult to quantify.

the physical productivity of the means of production is only a necessary, and not a sufficient, condition for the payment of rent, interest and profits. It is the social fact of *ownership* which underpins property income of all types, and which establishes their underlying unity. It is thus, with the share of property income as a whole, that we are primarily concerned.

There is also the question of 'human capital'. It is sometimes claimed that this renders obscure the distinction between employment and property incomes, since labour income itself derives from the ownership of this type of property. The difficulty with this claim is that 'human capital' is quite unlike any other asset. It is inseparable from its owner, and cannot be transferred from one person to another nor pledged as security for loans. In this respect 'human capital' is *qualitatively* different from all other forms of property, and it seems appropriate to treat the entire income of skilled workers as employment income.

There is clearly a very close relationship between our two broad categories of *income source*, and the Marxian and neo-Keynesian emphasis on *class shares*. Under some circumstances the correspondence between them might be complete. This would be so if there existed only two, mutually exclusive, classes: a working class which owned no property and derived its income entirely from work, and a capitalist class whose income was obtained entirely from the ownership of property.

In reality the social structure of advanced capitalist countries is more complex than this. Later in this chapter we discuss the problems posed by the continued existence of a class of self-employed, independent proprietors. Even ignoring this factor, however, class polarisation along traditional Marxist lines may be absent.

It is possible, for example, that the ownership of property has become diffused among the population as a whole, so that most people obtain income *both* from employment *and* from the ownership of property, and a 'pure' working class no longer exists. We shall see in Chapter 6 (pp. 60–1) that this question gives rise to some interesting problems in the theory of income distribution. Its practical importance, though, seems to be slight.

11

In Britain the richest 1 per cent own at least one-quarter, and the top 5 per cent at least one-half, of total personal wealth. The distribution of income from property is even more unequal, the top 5 per cent receiving no less than 92 per cent of all property income ([2] p. 14 and p. 36). Clearly the great majority of the working population own very little property, and their income from that property is exceedingly small. Nor is there any strong evidence that these inequalities are decreasing ([2] p. 24). While inequality in both the ownership of wealth and the distribution of property income seems to be higher in Britain than in most other advanced capitalist countries, similar qualitative conclusions may be drawn about them all.

The identification of a 'pure' capitalist class also presents difficulties, especially in view of the separation of ownership and control in most large companies. The directors and senior managers of many huge corporations are not major shareholders, or substantial holders of property in any form. But as their salaries are attributable to the exercise of *control* over large agglomerations of wealth, there is clearly a sense in which they should be regarded as capitalists.

We have already seen, however, that top salaries form a quite small proportion of total income from employment. Any understatement of the property share on these grounds would be relatively minor. Thus, although the distribution of power is not identical with the distribution either of property or of income, these problems may for our present purposes safely be ignored.

There are sectors of the economy to which the distinction between labour and property incomes cannot readily be applied. One of these is the state sector, the entire product of which is, moreover, conventionally treated as labour income. There is very little justification for this procedure. It tends to confuse comparisons of relative shares between countries, since the relative size of the government sector varies from country to country. More significantly, it gives rise to an upward bias in the share of labour over time, since the relative economic importance of the state has been increasing. In principle, then, only the private sector of the economy is relevant for the study of income shares.

Within the private sector there exists a sizeable intermediate class of self-employed people, neither simply workers nor simply capitalists, who receive both labour and property income. And 'by and large, the evidence is heavily in favour of the conclusion that the share of compensation of employees in national income, like the share of employees in the total labour force, generally rises with a country's economic growth' ([56] p. 53). Conversely, both the proportion of the self-employed in the total occupied population and their share in national income decline as industrialisation proceeds. This is partly – but by no means wholly – due to the relative decline in agriculture, where self-employment is most important.

Difficulties then arise, if we are interested in changes in the distribution of income between labour and property in the very long run, when these structural changes are very important.[1] How can we tell whether the increase in 'the share of compensation of employees in national income' can be attributed in its entirety to the decline in self-employment, or whether there has been a shift away from property income *independently of and in addition to* this decline? There are three ways in which this question might be answered.

One solution might be to focus our attention exclusively on the *corporate* sector of the economy, where the self-employed are by definition absent. If the data do not permit this, we might concentrate on those industries where self-employment is of negligible importance. Many studies thus deal with manufacturing alone, or in conjunction with mining, transport, communications and public utilities.[2] Others simply exclude strongholds of the self-employed like agriculture, retail trade and professional services.

Alternatively, we might attempt to allocate the income of the self-employed between its assumed labour and property components. There are several ways in which this might be done [52]. We might impute to the self-employed the average income from employment in the corporate sector, and treat their

---

[1] *Mutatis mutandis*, what follows is equally applicable to cross-sectional comparisons of relative shares, at a point in time, between countries.

[2] Where, as in Britain, some of these sectors are nationalised, they should be omitted for the reasons already stated.

13

property income as a residual (the 'labour basis'). Or we might reverse this procedure, imputing to them the average rate of profit on capital in the corporate sector, treating the remainder of their income (if any) as employment income (the 'asset basis'). Or we could divide income from self-employment between labour and property in the same ratio as it is distributed in the corporate sector (the 'proportional basis'); or apply some other, arbitrary, ratio. Finally, we could completely ignore the property ownership of the self-employed and regard their entire income as labour income [51].

There is a third approach, which deals with the whole economy rather than the corporate sector alone, but which also dispenses with the need for any of these methods of imputation. The observed share of 'the compensation of employees' may be expressed as the product of two ratios. The first is the ratio of employees, n, to the total occupied population including the self-employed, $N > n$. The second is the ratio of the average income of employees, w, to national income per head of the occupied population, y. Thus,

$$\frac{W}{Y} = \frac{w}{y} \cdot \frac{n}{N},\qquad(1)$$

where W is total 'employee compensation', and Y is national income. We expect n/N to rise over time, so that, *ceteris paribus*, W/Y will also rise. Whether there has been a shift away from property to labour income *independently* of the decline in self-employment depends on the movement of w/y, the 'wage income ratio'.[1] Changes in w/y thus reflect 'pure' distributional shifts between labour and property income.

We conclude that it is meaningful to distinguish two income shares, which we have termed employment (labour) and property income; that this distinction bears considerable similarity to the Marxian and neo-Keynesian classification of income by class shares, but much less resemblance to neo-classical concepts of 'factor shares'; and that methods exist for abstracting from

[1] The term is taken from [11] where, however, w and n refer to manual workers only. A similar concept appears in the literature under many different labels; see, for example [36] where it is termed the 'pay-parity ratio'.

14

changes in the economic significance of the state and of the self-employed. In the next chapter we assess the empirical evidence on the employment and property shares. Succeeding chapters appraise the main theories of relative shares in the light of this evidence.

2 A Survey of the Evidence

In this chapter we survey the evidence on relative shares in advanced capitalist countries. Our emphasis will be on changes in income distribution over time, rather than on comparing the level of income shares in different countries at any point in time. Apart from such notable exceptions as [11] and [60], cross-sectional studies are not often found in the literature, and most empirical work has focused on the course of relative shares within individual countries. Although the reliability of the data inevitably deteriorates as we go further back in time, it is nevertheless easier to draw confident conclusions about the course of income shares in Britain or the United States between (say) 1900 and 1970, than to compare relative shares in the two countries at either of those dates. Most theoretical work, too, has been concerned with trends in income distribution over time.

Perhaps the most important source of interest in the problem as a whole has been the alleged constancy of relative shares. As Solow ([89] p. 618) observes, 'it has been widely believed that the share of the national income accruing to labour is one of the great constants of nature, like the velocity of light and the incest taboo'. Constancy may refer to an absence of year-by-year changes in relative shares, or to an absence of any time-trend over a longer period. More precisely, relative shares may be described as 'constant' if no *significant* changes can be observed. In its narrow, statistical sense, the meaning of significance is clear enough. But not all changes in shares which pass the relevant statistical tests would automatically be regarded as *economically* significant.

There is thus no single wholly satisfactory test of the notion that relative shares have been constant over time. The data do not speak for themselves. They have to be interpreted, and interpretations can, quite legitimately, differ. Conflicts of interpretation are the more likely if, as we have seen to be the case in the previous chapter, the 'labour' and 'property' shares may be defined in a variety of ways. But it is still possible to draw reasonably confident conclusions. The first section of this chapter reviews the literature on the cyclical behaviour of income shares, and the second section assesses the long-run evidence. In neither case is much support found for the constancy hypothesis, upon which further doubt is cast in the third section, which deals with the recent 'profits squeeze'. Our emphasis throughout is on Britain and the United States, which have most frequently been studied. Where we deal with other Western countries, we shall do so much more briefly.

First, a note is necessary on terminology. We adhere as closely as possible to the distinction between *wages* (the pay of manual workers), *employee compensation* (wages plus salaries; abbreviated to EC), and *labour income* (EC plus the imputed labour income of the self-employed). Similarly we distinguish *corporate profits*, *total profits* (corporate profits plus interest and rent) and *property income* (total profits plus the imputed property income of the self-employed).

CYCLICAL MOVEMENTS IN RELATIVE SHARES

This section is very brief, for rare unanimity prevails with respect to cyclical movements in income shares. For Britain, Phelps Brown and Hart [12], dealing with the period from 1870 to 1939, contrast salaries and rent, which comprise the 'stable sector', with wages and corporate profits, which make up the 'fluctuating sector'. The shares of salaries and rent moved counter-cyclically throughout this period, increasing in the slump and decreasing in the boom. The shares of wages and corporate profits took the opposite course, with the latter fluctuating more sharply. Thus, as Kalecki [44] had earlier observed, the *wage* share in aggregate income was roughly constant over the cycle. But the share of EC underwent pronounced counter-cyclical movements, so that the share of total profits (dominated by its corporate profits component) increased in years of upswing and decreased in the downswing.

The weaker cycles of the post-1945 period display a similar pro-cyclical oscillation in the share of corporate profits [83]. An almost identical picture emerges for the United States ([54], [85]). We may safely conclude that the EC share fluctuates counter-cyclically, while the shares of both corporate profits and total profits move in the opposite direction. It should be noted that 'the most volatile income element is corporate profits, while the other constituents of the income distribution are relatively much more stable' ([54] p. 233). It is probably also true that these patterns apply to the labour and property shares, with the labour share rising in the slump and falling in the boom, and the property share moving in the opposite manner. This aspect of the problem, however, has been studied less often.[1]

RELATIVE SHARES IN THE LONG RUN

For our present purposes, the 'long run' is simply the longest time-span for which comparable and reasonably reliable data are available. For Britain, this is roughly from 1860 to the present day. For the United States, most time-series of income distribution date from 1900, although more speculative data exist for 1850–1900. Apart from one very ambitious attempt to measure relative shares in France from 1798 [58], data in other countries rarely go back beyond 1875. A century is clearly long enough, however, to assess the evidence for secular constancy in relative shares. (Changes in shares after 1960 are discussed in the next section.)

Table 1 presents the long-run evidence for Britain; it is derived from Feinstein [24], updated by the present authors. The share of EC is seen to rise in two major displacements, the first being between 1910–14 and 1921–4, and the second between 1935–8 and 1946–9. Before 1910 corporate profits cannot be separated

[1] The cyclical imputation of self-employment income is especially sensitive to the method of imputation which is used [52], so that imputation is a less useful procedure over the cycle than it is in the long run.

TABLE 1

Income shares as a percentage of gross national product at factor cost, United Kingdom, 1860–9 to 1969–73

Years	Employee compensation (1)	Income from self-employment Farmers (2)	Income from self-employment Others (3)	Corporate profits (4)	Rent (5)	Total domestic profits (6)	Gross domestic product (7)	Net property income from abroad (8)	Gross national product (9)
1860–9	45·2	6·4	30·6		14·8		97·0	3·0	100
1870–9	45·2	4·5	32·1		13·7		95·5	4·5	100
1880–9	46·2	2·7	31·4		13·9		94·2	5·8	100
1890–9	48·0	2·4	30·8		12·5		93·8	6·2	100
1900–9	47·7	2·3	31·3		12·1		93·4	6·6	100
1910–14	47·3	2·5	13·7	17·1	11·0	28·1	91·6	8·4	100
1921–4	58·5	2·1	15·1	13·0	6·8	19·8	95·5	4·5	100
1925–9	58·1	1·3	14·8	12·5	7·5	20·0	94·2	5·8	100
1930–4	59·3	1·6	13·4	12·5	9·0	21·5	95·8	4·2	100
1935–8	58·9	1·6	11·6	15·0	8·8	23·8	95·9	4·1	100
1946–9	65·3	2·9	9·4	16·8	4·0	20·8	98·3	1·7	100
1950–4	65·3	2·8	7·8	18·0	3·9	21·9	97·9	2·1	100
1955–9	67·0	2·3	6·9	18·0	4·5	22·5	98·7	1·3	100
1960–3	67·4	2·1	6·3	17·9	5·1	23·0	98·8	1·2	100
1964–8	67·6		8·0	16·8	6·4	23·2	98·8	1·2	100
1969–73	68·9		9·0	13·2	7·6	20·8	98·7	1·3	100

Sources: 1860–9 to 1960–3 [24] adapted from table 1, pp. 116–17; 1964–8 and 1969–73, calculated by the present authors from [68] table 1.

from non-agricultural self-employment income. After 1921–4 the share of self-employment income declines steadily, and the share of corporate profits increases rather unsteadily. The rent share declines down to 1950–4, unsteadily but rapidly, and then begins to rise. The share of total profits – in this case corporate profits plus rent – drops very sharply between 1910–14 and 1921–4, and rather less sharply between 1935–8 and 1946–9; it rises in the 1920s and 1930s, and again in the 1950s, and if anything displays an increasing long-run trend after 1921–4.

From 1910–14 onwards, Feinstein imputes the income of the self-employed on the 'labour basis' (see above, pp. 13, 14) but treats the entire income of professional people as labour income. He finds that the labour component of total self-employment income has risen steadily, from about one-half in 1910–14 to nearly three-quarters in 1960–3 (see [24] table 4, p. 125). The relative shares of labour and property, after imputation, are shown in Table 2, as percentages of gross national product and gross domestic product (G.N.P. less net property income from

TABLE 2

The Distribution of income between labour and property,
United Kingdom, 1910–14 to 1969–73

Years (annual averages)	Percentage of gross national product		Percentage of gross domestic product	
	Labour	Property	Labour	Property
1910–14	55·3	44·7	60·2	39·8
1921–4	67·4	32·6	70·6	29·4
1925–9	66·4	33·6	70·5	29·5
1930–4	68·1	31·9	71·1	28·9
1935–8	67·1	32·9	70·0	30·0
1946–9	73·0	27·0	74·3	25·7
1950–4	72·1	27·9	73·7	26·3
1955–9	73·4	26·6	74·4	25·4
1960–3	73·6	26·4	74·5	25·5
1964–8	73·6	26·4	74·4	25·6
1969–73	75·6	24·4	76·6	23·4

Sources: 1910–14 to 1960–3 [24] table 5, p. 126; 1964–8 and 1969–73, calculated by King and Regan from [68] table 1, imputing 75 per cent of self-employment income to labour, and 25 per cent to property.

abroad). Table 2 reveals the same sharp displacements, centred on the two World Wars, which we saw in Table 1 to be a feature of the EC share, before imputation. As a further refinement, Feinstein excludes rents of dwellings from property income. This reduces the *level* of the property share, but has little effect on the *trend* of relative shares ([24] table 6, p. 128).

Thus, Feinstein has demonstrated that both the EC and the labour shares have increased substantially since 1910–14, and that the property share has declined accordingly. It is true that the share of total profits (column 6 of Table 1) appears to have been roughly constant since 1921–4. But this is relevant only if we impute *all* self-employment income to labour; and it would be difficult to justify such a procedure.

For the United States the foremost practitioner of imputation is Kravis ([52], [53]). His 'raw' data for the period from 1900–9 to 1954–63 are given in columns 1 to 6 of Table 3. (Note that Table 3 uses overlapping decades.) The shares of both EC *and* corporate profits show a rising trend; the self-employment (farm and non-farm) and rent shares are declining; and the interest share displays no obvious trend. The U.S. picture is thus rather more complicated than that drawn by Feinstein for Britain. The EC share reaches its peak in the 1930s, and this huge increase in the great depression (for which there is no parallel in the British data) seems to have been much greater than that centred on the First World War. After 1930–9, moreover, the EC share is at best constant. Column 7 shows the course of the total profits share, which declines slightly between 1910–19 and 1920–9, and much more sharply between 1920–9 and 1930–9, but has no clear trend thereafter.

Columns 8 to 10 of Table 3 show the property share, calculated according to the 'asset', 'labour' and 'proportional' bases of imputation (see above, pp. 13, 14). Although the *level* of the property share is quite different in each column, the *trends* are very broadly the same.[1] They are in general agreement, moreover, with the 'raw' shares of EC (column 1) and total profits (column 7). The property share is unequivocally lower in

[1] This increases one's confidence in imputation as a general procedure, and also suggests that Feinstein's broad conclusions would probably have been unaffected had he used alternative bases for imputation.

TABLE 3

Income shares, overlapping decades, United States, 1900–9 to 1954–63

Years	Employee compensation (1)	Self-employment income Farm (2)	Non-farm (3)	Corporate profits (4)	Interest (5)	Rent (6)	Total profits (7)	Property income imputed on Asset basis (8)	Labour basis (9)	Proportional basis (10)
1900–9	55·0	11·6	12·1	6·8	5·5	9·0	21·3	30·6	32·2	32·1
1905–14	55·2	11·4	11·6	6·9	5·8	9·1	21·8	31·2	32·8	32·9
1910–19	53·6	11·7	12·1	9·1	5·4	8·1	22·6	32·6	35·8	34·8
1915–24	56·9	9·7	11·5	8·9	5·3	7·7	21·9	31·0	32·4	31·8
1920–9	60·8	7·2	10·3	7·8	6·2	7·7	21·7	29·2	28·5	28·8
1925–34	64·5	6·1	9·3	5·0	8·7	6·4	20·1	26·4	26·4	25·3
1930–9	67·5	6·0	8·8	4·0	8·7	5·0	17·7	22·9	19·8	21·4
1929–38	66·6	6·2	9·3	4·3	8·9	4·6	17·8	22·6	19·8	22·0
1934–43	65·1	6·6	9·9	9·1	6·0	3·3	18·4	23·6	23·5	22·9
1939–48	64·6	6·9	10·3	11·9	3·1	3·3	18·3	23·5	25·6	24·0
1944–53	65·6	6·4	10·0	12·5	2·1	3·4	18·0	23·1	24·7	23·6
1949–58	67·3	4·5	9·3	12·5	2·9	3·4	18·8	23·0	22·7	23·2
1954–63	67·9	3·2	8·7	11·2	4·0	3·0	18·2	n.a.	20·6	21·8

Source: [53] table 1, p. 134. Column 7 is the sum of columns 4, 5 and 6.

1954–63 than in 1900–9, and the labour share correspondingly higher. But – in contrast to the evidence for Britain – the data suggest virtual constancy in relative shares in the United States between the 1930s and the early 1960s.

In the previous chapter we suggested the calculation of wage income ratios as an alternative to imputation in dealing with self-employment income. Phelps Brown and Browne [11] derive, for Britain, the United States, Germany and Sweden, wage income ratios over the period from the late nineteenth century to the 1950s. Some of the shorter-term movements identified by Phelps Brown and Browne are rather surprising,[1] but the long-term trends revealed in Table 4 give considerable

TABLE 4

Long-run trends in the wage income ratio, four countries

	Britain	United States	Germany	Sweden
Period one (pre–1914)				
Span begins	1870	1889	1880	1870
Wage income ratio	63:73	59:71	62:67	51:67
Period two (1920–38)				
Span begins	1924	1920	1925	1920
Wage income ratio	68:71	68:80	62:64	56:62
Period three (1950–60)				
Wage income ratio	76:82	71:76	70:81	50:62

Source: adapted from [11] table 32, p. 335. Figures are the highest and lowest values of seven-year moving averages (periods one and two), and annual entries (period three). They refer to the 'industrial sector' (mining, manufacturing, transport, public utilities and construction); for Britain in period two, and the United States in periods one and two, they refer to manufacturing only.

---

[1] Notably the sharp increase in the British wage income ratio in the 1870s, and its equally sharp decrease in the 1880s and 1890s; and the very substantial decline in the later 1930s ([11] fig. 20, p. 135; fig. 40, p. 248). These are seven-year moving averages, and thus reflect something more than the normal cyclical fluctuations. It is difficult to see how they can be reconciled with the apparent stability in income distribution suggested by Tables 1 and 2 for these periods.

support to the conclusions of Feinstein and Kravis. Note that the wage income ratios of Table 4 relate to *wages* only, excluding salaries, and to the industrial sector only (as defined in the note to the table). They represent the highest and lowest values of the wage income ratio within each period.

Only for Sweden is there no evidence of any upward trend over the three periods. For the other three countries, the post-1945 wage income ratio is substantially higher than it had been before 1914. In the United States the increase occurred in its entirety between the first and second periods, in accordance with the pattern suggested by Table 3. In Germany, the increase occurred entirely between the second and third periods. The British case is more ambiguous. There is some evidence of an increase between 1914 and 1924, but the increase between the second and third periods is very much greater. Thus, Table 4 and Tables 1 and 2 tell a significantly different story. This puzzle is probably explained in part by the omission of salaries in [11], but it is doubtful whether this is the only factor involved. We should not in any case expect identical results from different data handled in quite distinctive ways.

For Britain the evidence of a long-run increase in the labour share is very convincing. Considerable doubt still exists, however, in the case of the United States. This is especially true if the problem of self-employment income is avoided by concentrating on predominantly corporate sectors of the economy. Thus, Loftus [60] found that the share of EC in value added in U.S. manufacturing was almost identical in 1889 and 1965, a conclusion supported by Lebergott [57]. We have already seen that any increase in either the EC or the labour share must have occurred before 1939. Even this is uncertain. Keller [48] found a declining EC share in manufacturing, transport, mining and utilities in the 1920s, while Grant [31] suggests that the share of EC in business product[1] was stable between 1899 and 1929. Thus, the bulk of the increase in the labour share seems to have occurred in the single decade of the 1930s.

Further studies in Sweden and West Germany, however, support Phelps Brown and Browne. Thalberg [92] reports

[1] Net national product minus household and government income and the external sector.

24

approximate stability in both the EC and labour shares in Sweden between 1870 and 1950; the labour share in industry actually declined. Jeck [39] provides data for Germany, where the EC share rose between 1875 and 1913, and again more rapidly until 1931, dropping substantially during the Nazi era and then recovering after 1945. The underlying trend is clearly upwards, and the same is true of the German wage income ratio until about 1925. After 1950 both Jeck and Heidensohn and Zygmant [36] agree that the wage income ratio has been declining.

For France, Lecaillon [58] reports a rising EC share from 1788 until 1914, constancy between the wars, and a continued increase since 1945. He argues, without providing detailed evidence, that this is not entirely accounted for by the decline in self-employment, so that the labour share too was increasing. Okhawa's [71] data for Japan show the EC share in the corporate sector taking an erratic course: constant at about 70 per cent between 1919 and 1931, declining to 56 per cent by 1938, rising dramatically to 90 per cent at the end of the war, and declining to the original 70 per cent by 1962. After using the 'labour basis' to impute self-employment income, Okhawa found no clear secular trend in the labour share.

Both Goldberg [30] and Kumar [55] agree that the labour share in Canada has been roughly constant since 1926, the increase in the EC share being largely attributable to the decline in self-employment (especially in agriculture). Budd [13], however, interprets Goldberg's data as revealing an *increasing* labour share, since there is a significant increase in the EC share in both manufacturing and in a wider 'predominantly corporate' sector,[1] where income from self-employment was of negligible importance. Finally, Woodfield [98] reports a declining EC share in New Zealand manufacturing between 1926 and 1966.

This section is not easy to summarise. In almost all the countries where data exist before 1914, the EC share shows a distinct upward trend [56]. With regard to the labour share, however, the position is more complicated. We can be fairly confident that the labour share has increased over the long

[1] Manufacturing, mining, transport, communications, utilities, finance, insurance and real estate.

period in Britain and Germany, and perhaps also in France. It is also safe to conclude that the labour share in Sweden has been roughly constant. The United States remains a puzzle. It is generally agreed that the labour share did not increase significantly between the 1930s and the early 1960s. There is a conflict of evidence concerning the first three decades of the century, imputation and wage income ratios suggesting an increasing labour share which is not apparent in studies of predominantly corporate sectors of the U.S. economy.

Data for other countries are not available before 1919. The share of labour in Canada may have increased since 1926, although probably not by very much. In Japan the absence of a clear trend in the labour share masks such huge fluctuations that it would be misleading to talk of 'constancy'. If the New Zealand manufacturing sector is representative of the economy as a whole, the labour share there has actually declined since 1926.

On balance the hypothesis of long-run constancy in relative shares must be rejected. In most cases the labour share was higher (and the property share lower) by 1960 than it had been at the turn of the century. Increasing labour shares are thus more common than either constant or decreasing shares, a conclusion supported for a more recent 'long run' by Heidensohn's [35] study of relative shares in seventeen countries between 1938 and the early 1960s.

THE RECENT 'PROFITS SQUEEZE'

Many authors agree that the last ten years have seen a dramatic shift from property to labour. Glyn and Sutcliffe ([29] table 3.2, p. 58) show the share of corporate profits in the net output of British companies declining gradually throughout the 1950s and early 1960s, and then dropping rapidly after about 1964. Their conclusions are supported by a careful reworking of the data by Burgess and Webb [14]. Thirlwall [93] reports an increase in the EC share between 1948 and 1969 in almost every sector of the British economy. Additional confirmation is provided by Heidensohn and Zygmant [36], according to whom a steady increase in the wage income ratio since 1950 appears to accelerate in the 1960s.

But this undeniable decline in the share of corporate profits has *not* been reflected in an equivalent decline in the shares of total profits or property as a whole, as may be seen from the present authors' calculations of these shares for 1964–8 and 1969–73 (Tables 1 and 2 above). The relative decline of corporate profits has been partially offset by a sharp increase in the share of rent, so that there has been a redistribution of income *within* the property share of no lesser importance than the shift from property as a whole to labour.

Glyn and Sutcliffe suggest that the profits squeeze is an international phenomenon, although some of their evidence for other Western economies is rather weak ([29] pp. 73–101). Convincing evidence of a recent shift to labour in the United States is, however, provided by Thirlwall, and also by Nordhaus [69]. For Germany, on the other hand, Heidensohn and Zygmant [36] show that the wage income ratio has been constant, with perhaps a slight downward tendency, since 1956.

CONCLUSION

In this chapter we have seen that the labour share fluctuates over the trade cycle, in the opposite direction to that taken by the level of economic activity (first section). It shows more signs of increasing than of remaining constant in the long run (second section), and it has risen significantly, if less dramatically than is often suggested, in Britain and the United States over the last decade (third section). The weight of the evidence clearly refutes the claim that labour's share is a constant. The following chapters outline some of the more important theories of relative shares, and assess their ability to explain our broad empirical conclusions.

3 Marginal Productivity Theory

Marginal productivity theory is a microeconomic theory of functional (not class) shares under conditions of perfect competitition in both product and factor markets, given technology, input supplies and consumer preferences. In its simplest form where there is only one commodity, it reduces to an explanation of functional shares in terms of input supply conditions and technology only.

Under perfectly competitive conditions, individual firms are price-takers in both factor and product markets and profit-maximising behaviour induces them to employ inputs until the long-run equilibrium rate of reward of each input is equal to its marginal physical product valued at the output price (i.e. to the value of its marginal product). This 'Law of Marginal Productivity' (Hicks [37] p. 9) is simply a consequence of profit maximisation under perfectly competitive conditions (see Mathematical Appendix, section A).

For individual firms facing given input prices, marginal productivity theory represents a theory of employment. When input supplies are fixed, it provides a theory of input rewards and thus of distribution.

We consider only the case of perfect competition in this chapter and defer discussion of non-perfect competition until Chapter 5.

EARLY APPROACHES

Marginal productivity theory was developed in the nineteenth century as an extension of marginal utility value theory to input prices. Even earlier, classical economics derived both distributive shares and commodity values from the rates of reward of the inputs. The Ricardian model of distribution in the agricultural sector is illustrated in Fig. 1, which follows Kaldor [41]. On the vertical axis is measured the output of corn, and on the horizontal axis inputs of labour-and-capital applied in fixed proportions to a given area of agricultural land. Labour-and-capital are treated as a single composite input, since they are

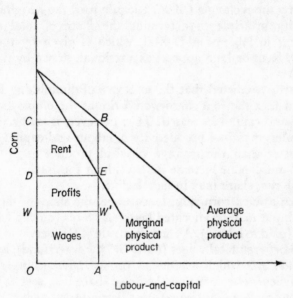

FIG. 1 *The Ricardian corn model*

perfectly complementary, a fixed amount of capital being used with each labourer. 'Capital' consists solely of a wage-fund of corn used to support labourers during the period of production, so that corn appears as both input and output; and appears, moreover, as the *only* input (other than labour and land). There is no fixed capital.

The size of the corn wage-fund, together with the long-run subsistence wage (also measured in terms of corn), determine both capital per labourer and the number of labourers employed. Once the quantity of labour-and-capital is determined at OA, and assuming that successive increments of labour-and-capital applied to the fixed area of land yield successively smaller increments of corn output, it is possible to determine the relative shares in output of land and labour-and-capital. In the case illustrated in Fig. 1, the marginal physical product of labour-and-capital lies below the average physical product, as both continually decline as increasing quantities of the composite input are employed. The total output of corn at OA is given by the rectangle $OABC$. Ricardo used the marginal productivity principle to determine the share of total output accruing to labour-and-capital, which is given by the area $OAED$. Rent on land appears as a residual, shown by the area $BCDE$.

Ricardo predicted that the existence of diminishing returns ensured that the rent share would rise as the employment of labour-and-capital increased. This, however, is *not* necessarily true unless marginal productivity of labour-and-capital *always* falls faster than the average physical product as inputs of capital-and-labour increase [62]. Without this further assumption the rent share may in fact decline.

Given a fixed corn subsistence wage, the share of the composite input may be allocated between profits (on capital) and wages (paid to labour). A corn wage rate of OW serves to divide $OAED$ between total wages ($OAW'W$, the wage-fund), and the area $WW'ED$ which accrues as profits. Diminishing returns *are* sufficient to ensure that the wage share increases as inputs of labour-and-capital rise, at least beyond some point. With a fixed subsistence wage, total wages rise in proportion with inputs of labour-and-capital, while output increases only at a diminishing rate, and average physical product must eventually decline. In most cases, including that illustrated in Fig. 1, the profit share falls towards zero as capital accumulation proceeds and an increasing quantity of labour-and-capital is applied to a given area of land.

The Ricardian model uses a simple marginal productivity theory and an exogenously determined subsistence wage to make predictions about relative shares in the agricultural sector. Here, the marginal productivity principle is applied *only* to the valuation of the composite input labour-and-capital, and *not* to land or to labour and capital separately.

Subsequent developments in the marginal analysis of commodity prices led to its extension to input prices in general, Von Thünen's being the first attempt (see Leigh [59]). Menger used what amounts to consumer utility maximisation in the presence of fixed commodity supplies to determine the values of commodities, and then imputed values to inputs through their capacity to produce final output. Although deficient in many respects, and particularly in neglecting diminishing returns, his analysis led him to value inputs according to their marginal productivities ([91], ch. VI). Wicksteed further developed the theory, and in his 'Co-ordination of the Laws of Distribution' [97] demonstrated the compatibility of Ricardo's residual rent with the rewarding of land in accordance with its marginal productivity.

This, together with a review by Flux [28], opened the debate concerning the *Adding-Up Problem*, which poses a major challenge to the internal consistency of the theory. If input prices are equal to the values of their marginal products, total payments to inputs must add up to the value of the total output of the commodity they serve to produce. If this is not so, some input(s) must be receiving more or less than their marginal products valued at the output price.[1] By applying the marginal productivity principle to only *one* composite input rather than to *all* inputs, Ricardo avoided this issue: the share of labour-and-capital, determined by marginal productivity, plus the *residual* rent, will always equal the value of total output.

At the same time Clark, in a series of articles and in his *Distribution of Wealth* [17], produced a very complete statement of marginal productivity theory as a set of equilibrium conditions in a static, perfectly competitive world. He used two homogeneous and divisible inputs, regarding land as a special kind of fixed capital. As a consequence of competition among entrepreneurs and among the owners of inputs, input rewards are equated with the values of their marginal products, all income being divided between interest (profits) on capital, and

[1] See Mathematical Appendix, section B.

wages. Clark's assumption of homogeneous divisible inputs ensures that marginal products are determinate, as the composition of a fixed input can always be altered in response to the addition or withdrawal of a unit of a variable input.

Clark also gave neo-classical theory a normative or prescriptive role according to which purely competitive long-run equilibrium ensured distributive justice. He criticised Von Thünen and Böhm-Bawerk for their notion that intramarginal labourers are always exploited by being paid less than the value of their marginal products and argued that the marginal productivity principle determined the 'natural values' of input prices. Together with Douglas's [21] exposition of the assumptions of Clark's analysis – a formidable list – this undoubtedly contributed to its fall from favour, and to its choice as a straw man *par excellence* by the critics of neo-classical theory.

MODERN DEVELOPMENTS

While earlier formulations of marginal productivity theory had concentrated on its input pricing aspects only, Hicks ([37] p. 117) re-emphasised relative shares. He gave apparent precision to the theory by introducing the concept of elasticity of substitution, and applying it to an *aggregate* production function to generate predictions about relative shares in national income. In this section we first introduce the concept of elasticity of substitution defined in terms of *any* two-input–one-output production function, and later discuss the level of aggregation at which it may appropriately be used.

Along a single isoquant of a production function, elasticity of substitution is the relationship between proportional changes in the ratio of input quantities and proportional changes in the marginal rate of technical substitution between these inputs. Where capital, K, and labour, L, are the inputs, elasticity of substitution may be written as

$$\sigma = \frac{\text{percentage change in } K/L}{\text{percentage change in the marginal rate of technical substitution between labour and capital}}.$$

By maintaining the assumption of perfect competition made at the outset of this chapter and assuming constant returns to scale, the marginal rate of substitution can be replaced by the input–price ratio as input prices equal the values of their marginal products. Now the elasticity of substitution can be written as

$$\sigma = \frac{\text{percentage change in } K/L}{\text{percentage change in } P_L/P_K}$$

and represents an index of the stability of relative input shares in the value of total output as the relative prices or quantities of the inputs vary. Furthermore, under constant returns to scale, the relationship between the capital–labour ratio and the marginal rate of technical substitution is the same along all isoquants. Elasticity of substitution need no longer be restricted to a single isoquant.

If constant returns to scale are not present, the adding up problem is not solved and some input(s) must receive more or less than the values of their marginal products. We cannot guarantee that the proportions by which input prices differ from the values of their marginal products will be the same for both inputs. Therefore, the marginal rate of technical substitution cannot be replaced by an input–price ratio.

But when these conditions are satisfied, the elasticity of substitution, as an index of the ease with which one input may be substituted for another, does yield predictions about relative shares in the value of output. If and only if $\sigma = 1$, any percentage change in the relative quantity of capital, K/L, results in an exactly equal percentage change in the relative price of labour, (P_L/P_K). If the relative quantity of capital rises (falls), it will be exactly offset by an equal percentage fall (increase) in the relative price of capital, so that the share of each input in the value of total output remains constant. Similarly, if the relative price of an input changes, a corresponding adjustment in input quantities would leave input shares unchanged.

If, however, $\sigma > 1$, an increase in the relative quantity of an input will induce an *increase* in its share, as a less than proportional increase in the relative price of the other input takes place. Conversely, if $\sigma < 1$, an increase in the relative quantity of an input *reduces* its share. Analogously, results can be derived for

changes in input prices such that an increase in the relative price
of an input *reduces* its share if $\sigma > 1$, and *increases* its share if $\sigma < 1$.

We have used the elasticity of substitution to predict changes
in shares: but shares of what? If, like Hicks, we wish to use it
to make predictions about shares in national income, we must
construct an aggregate production function for the whole
economy, and define elasticity of substitution in terms of it. This
generates severe logical problems, as we shall shortly see. For
the present we prefer to consider the elasticity of substitution
at a lower level of aggregation, where the concept of a production function is well-founded. We discuss aggregation problems
in the final section of this chapter.

Under perfect competition we begin at the level of the
industry. Individual firms will not be subject to variations in the
quantities of inputs available, since they all face perfectly
elastic input supply curves; and changes in input prices (shifts
in input supply curves) affect each firm equally. In long-run
equilibrium the industry will in fact operate under constant
returns to scale, since all firms will produce at minimum long-
run average cost, changes in industry output coming about
through changes in the number of firms via entry and exit. In
every firm both inputs will be paid the values of their marginal
products, and the elasticity of substitution can be used to predict
the effect of changes in relative input prices on the share of each
input in the value of the industry's output, as outlined above.[1]

Suppose, however, that the absolute price of labour increases.
It is not possible to predict the effect on relative shares of a rise
in the price of one input unless we know the impact of that
increase on *relative* input prices. But an increase in the absolute
price of an input does *not* entail that its relative price will also
rise. In fact, an increase in the price of one input will affect the
demand for, and hence possibly the price of, the *other* input in
two ways ([79] p. 259). First, depending on the elasticity of
substitution, there will be an *increase* in the demand for capital
because of substitution in production of capital for labour.
Secondly, depending on the price elasticity of demand for the
industry's product, the demand for capital will *decrease* as the

[1] Outside perfect competition none of these conclusions necessarily holds,
as will be shown in Chapter 5.

34

price of labour, and hence the price of output, goes up. On balance the demand for capital may rise, fall or (conceivably) remain constant. Depending upon this, and upon the elasticity of supply of capital to the industry, the price of capital may rise or fall as the price of labour increases.

The absolute and relative prices of an input can, however, be shown to vary in the same direction as long as the supply curve of the other input is not downward-sloping, and the demand curve for the product is not upward-sloping (see Hahn [32] but beware of misprints). Given these conditions, simple qualitative predictions can be made concerning the behaviour of relative shares in the value of a perfectly competitive industry's output as absolute input prices vary. But, if precise *quantitative* predictions are required, exact information about input supply elasticities and the elasticity of output demand is essential. Thus, knowledge of the elasticity of substitution alone is *not* sufficient to determine the precise effects of input price (or quantity) changes on relative shares in the value of the output of a perfectly competitive industry.

Technical change introduces further complications. In comparing different long-run equilibrium states of a perfectly competitive industry, it cannot generally be assumed that techniques are identical in each case. Hicks himself ([37] p. 121) introduced a simple classification of technical change. In a two-input production function of the type which we have been discussing, technical change is

(*a*) *neutral* if it raises the marginal products of both inputs in equal proportions;

(*b*) *labour-saving* if it raises the marginal product of capital relative to the marginal product of labour; and

(*c*) *capital-saving* if it raises the marginal product of labour relative to the marginal product of capital;

referring in each case to a *constant K/L ratio*.[1]

[1] For detailed discussion, see Hahn and Matthews [33], who also deal with the alternative classification of technical change proposed by Harrod. It should be noted that if technical changes must be 'embodied' in qualitatively different new machines, and if the industry's stock of machinery contains different 'vintages', our assumption of input homogeneity no longer holds. Some of the implications of this conclusion are discussed below.

Neutral technical change will clearly have no effect on relative shares, since the ratio of the marginal product of capital to that of labour (and hence the ratio of the input prices) is unchanged: in this case neither relative input quantities nor relative input prices have altered. But non-neutral or biased technical change must affect relative shares. Labour-saving changes increase the ratio of the marginal product of capital. to that of labour, so that, given K/L, the share of capital *increases*. Capital-saving technical change has the opposite effect.

Thus, in comparing different long-run equilibrium states of a perfectly competitive industry, three pieces of information are necessary to explain variations in relative shares: relative input prices (or quantities); the elasticity of substitution; and the direction of bias in technical change. Models of innovation *induced* by relative input price changes have been used to predict the direction and degree of bias, but with little success (see Bronfenbrenner [6] pp. 159–62). One can merely try to infer the bias involved by examining past behaviour of relative income shares, the elasticity of substitution and input prices and quantities.

There is a further problem relevant to the use of the elasticity of substitution which we have so far ignored. Even if we maintain the assumption of a single perfectly competitive industry, it is unlikely that the industry will employ only two inputs. It will normally use many different types of labour and capital, which therefore cannot be treated as single, homogeneous inputs. In this case the elasticity of substitution loses its neat symmetry, and has to be defined separately for each input.

Champernowne [16] has shown that in such circumstances the elasticity of substitution between any pair of inputs must be defined in terms of elasticities of substitution between *all pairs* of inputs. Hicks ([37] p. 378) concludes: 'I shall be careful to abstain from writing out an "elasticity of substitution" theory for more than two factors; nothing is to be gained by littering the page with determinants of second derivatives, the meaning of which it would be hard to disentangle.' He restricts himself instead to setting out the conditions under which all inputs can be treated as a single composite input like Ricardo's labour-

and-capital. Where there are many inputs and these conditions do not hold, the elasticity of substitution becomes unworkable.

AGGREGATION

All these reservations apply with equal force to the use of the elasticity of substitution with respect to an aggregate production function for the whole economy. *In addition*, further serious difficulties occur in the process of aggregation itself. The *Aggregation Problem* arises when attempts are made to apply an essentially *micro* relationship at a *macro* level, and to find appropriate macro variables. It is relatively easy to define the inputs and output of a single perfectly competitive industry, in which (subject to the problems encountered in the previous section) all firms produce the same homogeneous output using the same quantities of homogeneous inputs. When aggregating across industries, and not simply across firms within an industry, it cannot legitimately be assumed that inputs and outputs are homogeneous. Extremely strict conditions are required to permit the construction of an aggregate output index and similar input indices (see Fisher [26]).

In fact, aggregation is possible across many industries only if *all* the industry production functions are additively separable in their inputs. In the case of two inputs only (capital and labour) this means that the individual industry production functions contain *separate* terms in capital and labour so that the marginal product of capital is independent of the quantity of labour, and vice versa.

The main debate concerning the use of aggregate production functions has centred around the problem of constructing aggregate capital indices (see Harcourt [34]) but aggregate indices of output and labour also require highly restrictive conditions (especially if human capital is introduced). Walters [95] concludes: 'After surveying the problems of aggregation, one may easily doubt whether there is much point in employing such a concept as an aggregate production function.' We too consider that the use of an aggregate production function is not appropriate unless defined over a relatively homogeneous sector of the economy.

For the economy as a whole, aggregation problems simply do not permit the construction of indices of aggregate capital, labour and output. It follows that elasticity of substitution cannot be applied to the analysis of aggregate shares in national income. The problem is not merely one of *bias*, which results from the use of inappropriate aggregate indices, but concerns the *meaning* of the aggregate concepts.

In a static, perfectly competitive world, neo-classical theory does not permit simple predictions to be made concerning relative shares in national income. Even if elasticity of substitution *could* be defined at an aggregate level, it would no longer be a purely technological index, as *consumers* can be expected to substitute one commodity for another as input prices vary (Hicks [37]). Furthermore, although the effect of substitution between commodities as input prices change is determinate, it is not possible to predict the effect which input price changes have on commodity demand functions through their effects on consumers' incomes.

We may conclude this section as follows. As a microeconomic theory of input pricing in perfect competition, and with two inputs only, neo-classical theory allows simple statements to be made concerning the distribution of the value of an industry's output. With many inputs, or at an aggregate macro level, no clear statements can be made.

Deviations from *either* perfect competition *or* from equilibrium may destroy even these very limited conclusions. These additional problems are considered in Chapter 5.

4 Marginal Productivity: The Econometrics

This chapter discusses the use of marginal productivity theory in the context of aggregate production functions estimated from empirical observations.

THE COBB–DOUGLAS PRODUCTION FUNCTION

The Cobb–Douglas production function has proved to be the most widely used of all the production functions estimated from aggregate data. A function of the Cobb–Douglas type was first introduced by Wicksell but Cobb and Douglas began its great popularity. In 1928 [18] they used a function of the form $Q = AL^\alpha K^\beta$ to explain Douglas's time-series data for American manufacturing industry. In this function, Q represents output, L labour, K capital and A is a constant term reflecting the productivity of both inputs.

The extraordinary popularity of the Cobb–Douglas production function may be partly explained by its convenient mathematical properties. If it is assumed that input marginal products have the same meaning in an aggregate *macro* Cobb–Douglas production function as those of a similar *micro* function, simple predictions about relative shares can be derived.

If the existence of perfect competition guarantees the equality of input prices (measured in terms of the single output) with their marginal physical products, the Cobb–Douglas function generates constant relative shares. Formally,

$$Q = AL^\alpha K^\beta \qquad (2)$$

marginal product of $L = \dfrac{\delta Q}{\delta L} = \alpha A L^{\alpha-1} K^\beta = \alpha \dfrac{Q}{L}, \qquad (3)$

marginal condition $\qquad w = a \dfrac{Q}{L},$ $\qquad\qquad$ (4)

total labour income $\qquad wL = aQ,$ $\qquad\qquad\qquad$ (5)

labour's share $\qquad\qquad \dfrac{wL}{Q} = a.$ $\qquad\qquad\qquad$ (6)

Similarly, capital's share in total output can be shown to be β and both are independent of the capital–labour ratio. The function, therefore, predicts *constant* relative shares, or, expressed another way, the Cobb–Douglas function has an elasticity of substitution of unity (see above, pp. 32–4, and Mathematical Appendix, section C).

It can be seen that if and only if $\alpha + \beta = 1$ relative input shares will add up to total output. The sum of the exponents, in fact, determines the type of returns to scale exhibited by the function. $\alpha + \beta = 1$ implies constant returns to scale (see Mathematical Appendix, section B). If $\alpha + \beta > 1$ then equal proportional increases in both inputs can be shown to increase output *more* than proportionally. In this case, input rewards will more than exhaust total output. Conversely, $\alpha + \beta < 1$ implies diminishing returns to scale and underexhaustion of total output. To re-iterate an important point: the adding up problem (see above, p. 31) is solved if and only if $\alpha + \beta = 1$.

Although the Cobb–Douglas production function is not linear, it can be made linear, and therefore easier to estimate, by rewriting it in logarithms:

$$\log Q = \log A + \alpha \log L + \beta \log K. \qquad\qquad (7)$$

It seems that, in this form, it satisfies the conditions for aggregation (see above, pp. 37, 38) as the logarithms of capital and labour appear in separate terms. This is not so, however, because if all the micro production functions are of Cobb–Douglas form, the *macro* function will be of the same form but defined in terms of geometric means of the data.[1]

---

[1] The micro functions are of the form:

$$\log Q_i = \log A_i + \alpha \log L_i + \beta \log K_i.$$

Summing $\displaystyle\sum_{i=1}^{N} \log Q_i = N \log A + \alpha \sum_{i=1}^{N} \log L_i + \beta \sum_{i=1}^{N} \log K_i,$

EMPIRICAL ESTIMATES OF THE COBB–DOUGLAS FUNCTION

Cobb and Douglas [18] first estimated their production function using time-series data for American manufacturing industry between 1889 and 1922. The data consisted of index numbers of physical output, the dollar value of fixed capital and the number of workers employed. They first used the function in its constant returns to scale form[1] but later estimated α and β separately using an equation of the form (7). Their initial results gave a good statistical fit and an estimated α of 0·75 which corresponded very closely with labour's *actual* share in manufacturing of 74 per cent in the decade 1909–18.

In later time-series studies where the sum of exponents was not restricted to unity, Cobb and Douglas found a tendency for the labour exponent to over-estimate labour's actual share and for a corresponding underestimation of capital's share. Nevertheless, the exponents did sum to near unity suggesting roughly constant returns to scale.

Cobb and Douglas also undertook interindustry cross-sectional studies for American manufacturing. Douglas reported the results of six such studies in 1948 [22].

The six studies, using data for selected years between 1889 and 1919, yielded sums of exponents near unity but the values of α and β varied considerably from one study to the next. By

---

which may be divided by N (the number of firms or industries) to give an average function:

$$\log \text{g.m.} (Q) = \log A + \alpha \log \text{g.m.} (L) + \beta \log \text{g.m.} (K),$$

where g.m. represents a geometric mean (see Murti and Sastry [66]).

[1]
$$Q = AL^{\alpha}K^{1-\alpha},$$
$$\frac{Q}{K} = AL^{\alpha}K^{-\alpha},$$
$$\frac{Q}{K} = A\left[\frac{L}{K}\right]^{\alpha};$$

in logs
$$\log\left[\frac{Q}{K}\right] = \log A + \alpha \log\left[\frac{L}{K}\right];$$

in this case α can be estimated using simple regression.

taking averages of the values of α and β from these studies, Douglas calculated a labour exponent of 0·63 and a capital exponent of 0·34 which corresponded very well with an observed labour share in manufacturing of 60·5 per cent. Furthermore, by removing time trends from the data, the time-series estimates of relative shares could be made consistent with the observed shares. Douglas interpreted this American evidence, together with the results of studies in other countries, as support for marginal productivity theory and the Cobb–Douglas production function. We suggest below that the evidence cannot be interpreted in this manner.

More recent interindustry cross-sectional studies of the Cobb–Douglas production function have predicted relative shares fairly well (see Walters [95]) but time-series studies have produced some unusual results. Time-series studies using data for the 1920s and 1930s have produced some striking overestimates of labour's share (with $\alpha > 1$!) and increasing returns to scale probably as a result of the underutilisation of inputs. In such periods, the input indices have been unable adequately to reflect variations in the intensity with which the inputs are used.

OBJECTIONS TO THE COBB–DOUGLAS FUNCTION

Fundamental objections to *any* aggregate production function have already been raised when considering the question of aggregation (see above, pp. 37, 38) but, even if aggregation problems are swept under the carpet, grave doubts still exist concerning the *meaning* of the Cobb–Douglas function when fitted to aggregate data.

First, lack of data forces investigators to use only very rough indices of output and the flows of factor services. Capital, labour and output are difficult to measure as all three are subject to wide variations in quality and, therefore, require some form of weighting in order to construct aggregate indices. Capital measurement problems can be extremely intractable and have received most attention in the literature (for extensive discussion see Harcourt [34]). Most studies use an index of capital stock rather than the flow of capital services and experience great difficulty in allowing for depreciation and incorporating the effects of technical progress which is embodied in new capital equipment. Furthermore, the input indices are unable fully to incorporate variations in the intensity with which labour and capital are used. For both cross-sectional and time-series studies of aggregate production functions, the nature of the data available raises doubts as to the meaning of the results obtained.

Secondly, and even if all the aggregation and data problems did not exist, it may still be the case that studies fitting Cobb–Douglas aggregate production functions are not able to *identify* a production function at all. If technology is accurately represented by a Cobb–Douglas function, the coefficients estimated in an equation of the form (7) need not be those of the production function. When input prices stay constant, an equation of exactly the same form as (7) can be derived by combining the marginal productivity conditions of capital and labour (equations of the form (4)). We may simply estimate the coefficients of this derived equation rather than those of the production function. The identification problem is likely to be serious in interindustry cross-sectional studies as input prices may remain constant from one industry to another.

Thirdly, the apparent success of the fitted Cobb–Douglas aggregate production function need not be because perfect competition prevails and the function accurately represents technology. It may be because the Cobb–Douglas function closely approximates another relationship.

In interindustry cross-sectional studies, the correspondence between input shares and the estimated exponents of a Cobb–Douglas function cannot be taken as proof that technology is adequately described by the Cobb–Douglas form. Phelps Brown [8] has argued that this result may be derived from a cost function and not from a production function.[1] Simon and

---

[1] This proposition can be very simply demonstrated since with $\alpha + \beta = 1$ and in logarithms we can write a Cobb–Douglas function $\log (Q/K) = \alpha \log (L/K)$ for changes in the variables $d \log (Q/K) = \alpha \, d \log (L/K)$. *But*, a *cost* function, $Q = wL + rK$, can be written $Q/K = w(L/K) + r$. Assuming r and w stay constant,

$$d \, Q/K = w \, d \, (L/K),$$

Levy [87] later proved this proposition showing that a linear function of the form $Q = wL + rK$ could be well approximated by a Cobb–Douglas function. In this case, w is the wage rate and r the rate of profit or interest. A good statistical fit implies *nothing* about the validity of the marginal productivity theory of relative shares or the Cobb–Douglas function as a description of technology.

When using time-series data, Phelps Brown [8] has also demonstrated that the exponents of a Cobb–Douglas production function can be derived from the historical growth rates of output, labour and capital and not technology.[1] Again, the estimation of a Cobb–Douglas aggregate production may reveal nothing about marginal productivity theory or technology.

Fourthly, if the data on capital and labour are closely related in either cross-sectional or time-series studies, problems of *intercorrelation* may prevent us estimating α and β separately. In practice, however, correlation between the inputs has not been serious enough to prevent estimation of the exponents.

Finally, it is likely that the aggregate production function will shift upwards over time as a result of technical progress. Time-series studies, therefore, have to distinguish between shifts in

---

which may be written as

$$Q/K \, \mathrm{d} \log (Q/K) = L/wK \, \mathrm{d} \log (L/K).$$

Hence

$$\mathrm{d} \log (Q/K) = L/wQ \, \mathrm{d} \log (L/K),$$

where labour's share $Lw/Q = \alpha$.

[1] Using index numbers of inputs and output, if all three grow at constant proportional rates, we can write $\log Q = At$, $\log L = Bt$, $\log K = Ct$, where t denotes time. Using index numbers and in logs the Cobb–Douglas production function (in constant returns to scale form) can be written

$$\log Q = \alpha \log L + (1 - \alpha) \log K.$$

Substituting:
$$At = \alpha Bt + (1 - \alpha) \, Ct,$$
$$A = \alpha B + (1 - \alpha) \, C,$$
$$A - C = \alpha \, (B - C),$$
$$\frac{A - C}{B - C} = \alpha.$$

production functions and movements along them in order to estimate their parameters. The Cobb–Douglas production function can incorporate technical progress *only* through the term A. Technical progress which increases the value of A is *disembodied* as it is independent of the quantities of capital and labour and *neutral* as it raises the productivity of both inputs in equal proportions (see above, pp. 35, 36). Technical progress in a Cobb–Douglas production function will, therefore, have no effect on relative shares.

Solow [88] has devised a way of segregating shifts in an aggregate production function due to neutral technical progress from movements along such a function. He assumes that the production function (which need not be a Cobb–Douglas) has constant returns to scale and derives an equation of the form:

$$\dot{q}/q = \dot{A}/A + SK\, \dot{k}/k, \tag{8}$$

where $\dot{q}/q$ is the proportional rate of change of output per head, $\dot{k}/k$ is the proportional rate of change of capital per head, SK is capital's share and $\dot{A}/A$ is the proportional rate of neutral technical advance.[1] Using time-series data of output per man hour, capital per man hour and capital's share, he estimates $\dot{A}/A$ as a residual in equation (8). Finally, he uses the estimated technical progress term to weight the series of observations of

[1] $Q = A(t)\, f(K, L)$ where $A(t)$ represents neutral technical progress as a function of time. Taking time derivations and dividing by Q,

$$\frac{\dot{Q}}{Q} = \frac{\dot{A}(t)}{A(t)} + A(t)\frac{\partial f}{\partial K}\frac{\dot{K}}{Q} + A(t)\frac{\partial f}{\partial L}\frac{\dot{L}}{Q}, \qquad \dot{A}(t) = \frac{\partial A(t)}{\partial t}, \text{ etc.}$$

Capital's share
$$SK = \frac{MPK \times K}{Q} = A(t)\frac{\partial f}{\partial K}\frac{K}{Q},$$

therefore,
$$\frac{\dot{Q}}{Q} = \frac{\dot{A}(t)}{A(t)} + SK\frac{\dot{K}}{K} + WL\frac{\dot{L}}{L}.$$

But, $SK = 1 - SL$ as we have assumed constant returns to scale. Therefore,

$$\left[\frac{\dot{Q}}{Q} - \frac{\dot{L}}{L}\right] = \frac{\dot{A}(t)}{A(t)} + SK\left[\frac{\dot{K}}{K} - \frac{\dot{L}}{L}\right],$$

which can be rewritten

$$\dot{q}/q = \dot{A}/A + SK\,(\dot{k}/k).$$

45

output to remove the effects of shifts in the production function. A Cobb–Douglas function fitted to the data adjusted in this manner gives an almost perfect fit.

Despite the fact that there is some empirical support for neutral technical progress (see Kennedy and Thirlwall [49]), estimating $\dot{A}/A$ as a residual means that it may include almost anything. It represents a rag-bag possibly incorporating the effects of improvements in human capital, shifts of resources, economies of scale and errors in the measurement of inputs as well as technical progress. Residuals such as this invariably explain at least half the observed growth rate of output and have spawned numerous important studies attempting to evaluate the effects of technical progress, education, etc. Nevertheless, because many of the factors which raise input productivity, like education, training and technical progress, are interrelated, it has not been possible to estimate their effects separately.

If technical progress is neutral it will have no effect on relative shares (see above, pp. 35, 36). If, as seems likely, technical progress is not neutral and is *embodied* in the inputs, its effect on relative shares will depend on the elasticity of substitution. Embodied technical progress raises the effective quantities of the inputs as the input indices are replaced by weighted sums of capital and labour embodying different amounts of technical progress. In the Cobb–Douglas aggregate production function, shares will be unaffected by differences in the rates at which technical progress is embodied in labour and capital as the elasticity of substitution is unity. If elasticity of substitution is not unity, relative shares *will* change if embodied technical progress augments labour and capital at different rates and so changes the effective capital–labour ratio. We now consider aggregate production functions where the elasticity of substitution may differ from unity.

Before doing so, however, we conclude that, as a result of problems of aggregation, data and identification, together with the interpretation of technical progress, Cobb–Douglas production functions fitted to aggregate data tell us very little. A good fit does not constitute a test of either marginal productivity theory or the hypothesis that technology is described by a

Cobb–Douglas function. If there is *independent* evidence of perfect competition and many other problems can be overcome, fitted Cobb–Douglas production functions may describe technology. Otherwise they cannot. The success of the Cobb–Douglas function appears to be the result of the rough constancy of relative shares over long periods of time (see Fisher [27]). It does not demonstrate that roughly constant shares occur as a result of perfect competition and a Cobb–Douglas aggregate production function.

THE CONSTANT ELASTICITY OF SUBSTITUTION PRODUCTION FUNCTION

The constant elasticity of substitution (C.E.S.) aggregate production function, like the Cobb–Douglas, is based upon empirical observations. Its present popularity as an alternative to the Cobb–Douglas function began when it was fitted to inter-country cross-sectional data by Arrow *et al.* [1]. It may also offer an intuitively appealing explanation of the tendency of labour's share to rise if the elasticity of substitution is not one, but lies *below* unity while the capital–labour ratio has been rising. We discuss the C.E.S. function only briefly as, to date, the empirical evidence does not clearly confirm that the elasticity of substitution differs from unity and formal treatments are available elsewhere (see Bronfenbrenner [6] appendix to ch. 16 and [1]). If the elasticity of substitution is unity, the C.E.S. function simply reduces to the Cobb–Douglas form.

The C.E.S. production function can be written in the form

$$Q = A[bL^{-\alpha} + (1-b)K^{-\alpha}]^{-1/\alpha}, \qquad (9)$$

where Q, L and K represent output, labour and capital, respectively, and A and b are constants. Empirical tests have employed the function in this form where it exhibits constant returns to scale and, under conditions of perfect competition, the adding-up problem is solved (see Mathematical Appendix, section B). A is a scale or efficiency parameter of the same type as the constant term in a Cobb–Douglas function; b is the so-called distribution parameter, which, together with the capital–

labour ratio and α, determines relative shares. Lastly, α determines the elasticity of substitution of the C.E.S. function and is equal to $(1/\sigma) - 1$, where σ is the elasticity of substitution (see [6]).

On the assumption that perfect competition equates input prices (measured in terms of output) with their marginal physical products, a relationship between output per head and the wage rate can be derived from the C.E.S. function and used in empirical testing. Formally, marginal product of labour:

$$\frac{\partial Q}{\partial L} = A\left(-\frac{1}{a}\right)\left[bL^{-\alpha} + (1-b)K^{-\alpha}\right]^{-1/\alpha-1}b(-a)L^{-\alpha-1}, \quad (10)$$

$$= bA[bL^{-\alpha} + (1-b)K^{-\alpha}] - \left(\frac{1+a}{a}\right)L^{-(1+\alpha)}, \quad (11)$$

$$= \frac{b}{A^{\alpha}}\left(\frac{Q}{L}\right)^{1+\alpha} = w, \text{ under perfect competition,} \quad (12)$$

from which we derive:

$$\frac{Q}{L} = \left(\frac{A^{\alpha}}{b}w\right)\frac{1}{1+\alpha}.$$

In logs

$$\log\left(\frac{Q}{L}\right) = [\text{a constant}] + \frac{1}{1+a}\log w, \quad (13)$$

but, $1/(1+a) = \sigma$, the elasticity of substitution; therefore

$$\log\left(\frac{Q}{L}\right) = [\text{a constant}] + \sigma \log w. \quad (14)$$

A similar relation can be derived from the Cobb–Douglas function simply by rearranging equation (4) and writing it in logarithms:

$$\log Q/L = -\log a + \log W. \quad (15)$$

If elasticity of substitution is unity, equations (14) and (15) become identical.

The results of intercountry cross-sectional studies for a variety of industries (see [6]) do not yield estimates of σ which differ significantly from unity. Therefore, we cannot reject the Cobb–

Douglas function in favour of a constant return to scale C.E.S. aggregate production function with an elasticity of substitution which differs from unity.

The C.E.S. function is *theoretically* superior to the Cobb–Douglas as it can be made additively separable to overcome aggregation problems (see above, pp. 37, 38) and it is of a more general form which can incorporate the Cobb–Douglas function as a special case. There is no evidence, however, that it represents a better description of reality. Our earlier conclusions still stand. Cobb–Douglas or C.E.S. functions fitted to aggregate data do not confirm marginal productivity theory or the existence of a particular type of aggregate technology.

5 'Monopoly' and Relative Shares

The Polish economist Michal Kalecki made the first attempt to formalise the popular notion that the profit share depends on the degree of market power enjoyed by the firm. Kalecki's pioneering work was largely undertaken in the 1930s, and was deeply influenced by the climate of the times.[1] Neo-classical economists were confronted by two fundamental and interwoven challenges. The microeconomic paradigm of pure competition was seen to be increasingly irrelevant to the realities of modern capitalism; and the full employment of economic resources, on which neo-classical macroeconomics pivoted, had become a myth. The theoretical relationship between these two problems was simple. The widespread existence of excess capacity made it very probable that the firm faced constant or falling marginal costs; and this is incompatible with purely competitive equilibrium.

Reactions to these problems varied. It could be argued: (i) that pure competition was pervasive, but that equilibrium was not; (ii) that equilibrium was pervasive, but that pure competition was a special, and not the general, case; or (iii) that both conventional equilibrium analysis and the model of pure competition must be rejected. The first position had little to commend it. The second was adopted by theorists of 'monopolistic' [15] or 'imperfect' [79] competition, who applied the marginal productivity doctrine to departures from pure competition. When product demand curves are downward-sloping, marginal revenue is less than price, and the net addition to total revenue brought about by the employment of an

[1] His first exposition [44], published in 1939, was greatly improved in the 1954 version [45], and reprinted in [46], which we follow here.

additional unit of a factor – its marginal revenue productivity (*MRP*) – is less than the value of its marginal product (*VMP*). Factor pricing still depends on marginal productivity, but in a more complicated way (see Mathematical Appendix, section A).

This position involves a weakening of the apologetic role of marginal productivity theory, for now *no* profit-maximising firm will pay labour its *VMP*, and even on the Pigovian definition of exploitation workers will be exploited.[1] Moreover, the adding-up problem rears its head in a more intractable form. Since factor prices are inevitably less than their *VMPs*, and the existence of pure competition is denied, neither of Wicksell's two solutions to the problem can be applied. There are, however, analogies to both. We show in the Mathematical Appendix that the adding-up problem can be solved outside pure competition if the aggregate production function is homogeneous and displays increasing returns to scale *of a particular strength* which depends on the 'degree of monopoly' (on which, see below, pp. 52, 53). But this will occur, if at all, only by accident.

Similar to the second Wicksellian solution is the proposition that the universal existence of the 'tangency solution' – in which the demand curve is tangent, at the profit-maximising output, to the firm's average cost curve – also solves the adding-up problem. This entails that, in long-run equilibrium, all firms earn the same rate of profit; i.e. that the degree of market imperfection is the same in every industry. This is only a little more likely than the universal existence of pure competition. Thus, marginalist equilibrium theory is unable to provide a determinate theory of factor shares outside pure competition.

Kalecki took the third position, which is not open to these theoretical objections, and which also corresponds more closely to observed business behaviour. He distinguished between 'demand-determined' and 'cost-determined' processes. The former, relevant to agricultural production, are open to ortho-

[1] This is doubly true if the firm has *monopsonistic* power in its *labour* market, facing an upward-sloping labour supply curve. In this case the marginal cost of labour is greater than the wage. Since cost-minimisation requires that the firm equates the marginal cost of a factor with its *MRP*, the wage is less than the *MRP* of labour, and even further below its *VMP* [15].

dox marginalistic analysis; the latter, accounting for the remainder of the private sector, are not. Up to capacity output, Kalecki argued, the average variable cost (AVC) curve of the typical non-agricultural firm is approximately horizontal, and thus identical with its short-run marginal cost (SMC) curve. Since capacity output is rarely attained, even in boom conditions, this is in practice the only relevant section of the curve. Kalecki's model does *not*, therefore, apply to conditions of extreme demand pressure.

Kalecki suggests that the firm sets its price, p, not by equating marginal revenue (MR) with SMC, but by applying a mark-up, k (>1) to its AVC. Once arrived at, p is invariant with respect to all but the most drastic changes in demand. The procedure is thus not consistent with orthodox profit maximisation. It follows that

$$p = k \times AVC. \tag{16}$$

Denote the firm's total revenue (price times quantity) by R, its total wage bill by W, and its total expenditure on raw materials by M. The sum of W and M represents *total* variable cost, so that

$$R = k(W + M). \tag{17}$$

The difference between R and total variable costs represents overhead costs and net profits, so that

$$\text{overheads} + \text{net profits} = k(W + M) - (W + M) = (k - 1)(W + M). \tag{18}$$

For the economy as a whole, we may write *gross* national income, Y, as

$$Y = W + \text{overheads} + \text{net profits}, \tag{19}$$

where the terms on the right-hand side denote the sums of wages, overheads and net profits in every firm. If we write $M/W = j$, we can write the wage share in gross national income as

$$\frac{W}{Y} = \frac{W}{W + \text{overheads} + \text{net profits}} = \frac{W}{W + (k-1)(W + M)}$$

$$= \frac{1}{1 + (k-1)(j+1)}. \tag{20}$$

According to equation (20), the wage share is solely dependent on, and inversely related to, j and k.

If we assume that the physical input coefficients, per unit of output, of labour and raw materials are constant, j represents the relative *price* of raw materials in terms of labour. From equation (16), we know that $k = p/AVC$. Since Kalecki assumes that $AVC = SMC$, it follows that $k = p/SMC$. In pure competition, therefore, when $p = SMC$, k must equal unity. In all other types of product market k exceeds unity, and it seems reasonable to suppose that, the more 'monopolistic' the market, the greater is the gap between price and marginal cost, and hence the greater is k. Thus, k represents the 'degree of monopoly'.[1] Kalecki's analysis tells us that the wage share will be greater, the lower the price of raw materials in terms of labour, j, and the lower the degree of monopoly, k.

Kalecki found that the degree of monopoly in U.S. manufacturing was increasing over the long period from 1879 to 1937, and that an offsetting downward trend in j was insufficient to prevent a decline in the wage share. For the U.K. economy between 1881 and 1924 there was no significant trend in the wage share, despite a clear decline in j. Kalecki concluded that in Britain secular growth in the degree of monopoly had exactly offset the decline in j, leaving the wage share constant. In a cyclical context, he found that in both countries the wage share tended to remain constant throughout the great depression (1929 to 1937 or 1938): j declined in the slump and rose in the boom, while k took the opposite course, and the two movements cancelled each other out.

This interpretation of the historical record did not go unchallenged. Dunlop [23] claimed that the alleged cyclical constancy of the wage share in U.S. manufacturing masked sub-

---

[1] The degree of monopoly may alternatively be defined as $(k - 1) = (p - SMC)/SMC$. If we are willing to admit that firms act as neo-classical profit maximisers then, and *only* then, $SMC = MR$ and $(k - 1) = (p - MR)/MR$. Now $MR = p(1 - 1/e)$, where e is the price-elasticity of product demand [79]. Thus, $(k - 1) = 1/(e - 1)$, and the degree of monopoly varies inversely with the elasticity of demand. Although Kalecki flirted with this formulation in his earlier work, it must be repeated that his 1954 model [45] is a *disequilibrium* analysis which is inconsistent with this interpretation of the degree of monopoly.

stantial variations within individual industries, though in [45] pp. 34–6, Kalecki performs a shift-share analysis which appears to refute this criticism. Rostow [80] objected that in the United Kingdom the wage share rose between 1880 and 1900, and then declined until 1914, while the degree of monopoly followed the reverse course.[1] Various authors have observed that, while data existed for the 'ratio of proceeds to prime costs', k, in the United States, no such information was available for Britain, so that Kalecki's estimates of trends in the degree of monopoly in the United Kingdom were purely subjective.

In general, however, Kalecki's critics attacked the theoretical rather than the empirical structure of his model. Some of the criticisms miss the point. It is irrelevant to object, as does Bronfenbrenner ([6] p. 411), that in pure competition, where $p = SMC$, the wage share would equal unity and both gross and net profits would be zero. Kalecki is quite explicit that his model applies only to imperfect markets, and that an entirely different approach (which could not be based on a mark-up pricing procedure) would be required for the analysis of factor shares in pure competitiion. As pure competition is rarely encountered outside agriculture, his failure to provide such an analysis cannot be counted as a serious omission.

Greater problems are posed by Kalecki's treatment of salaries which, he mentions in a one-line footnote ([44] p. 12, n. 1), are included in overheads, and which thus form part of gross non-wage income. But there is no strong socio-economic basis for distinguishing between wage- and salary-earners, and it is preferable to take wages and salaries together in studying relative shares (see above, pp. 9, 10). Kalecki is unable to do this because of the importance which he attaches to the distinction between fixed and variable costs. But there is in reality both a variable element in the cost of salaried labour and a fixed element in the cost of manual labour [70]. It can thus be argued that both should be treated as 'quasi-fixed' factors, leaving only raw materials as a *purely* variable cost, and radically undermining the basis of Kalecki's model.

[1] In view of the large margins of error in the pre-1914 data ([24] pp. 136–7) it is doubtful whether any significant changes in the wage share actually occur.

54

Even ignoring salaries, serious doubts remain as to the meaning of any analysis conducted in terms of the aggregate degree of monopoly. Davidson ([19] p. 54) objects that 'defining the degree of monopoly as the ratio of aggregate proceeds to aggregate prime costs reduces it to a tautological explanation of class shares', while Bauer ([4] p. 199) dismisses the aggregate degree of monopoly as 'a meaningless portmanteau, very similar to the Velocity of Circulation'. Both authors regard equations (16) to (20) as *identities* which are true under all circumstances and therefore provide no *theory* of relative shares.

Despite the attempts of Riach [78] to defend Kalecki against these criticisms, they seem well-founded. Kalecki convincingly explains short-run variations in j in terms of the relative inelasticity of supply of primary products, but gives no account of the factors determining long-run changes in j (see [45]). His analysis of the determinants of k is piecemeal: defensive collusion in the slump gives rise to counter-cyclical fluctuations in the degree of monopoly, while in the long run growing industrial concentration and rising selling costs are partially offset by countervailing increases in trade union power ([45] and [47] both reprinted in [46]). Kalecki offers no evidence of these developments, although for some at least it could readily be obtained. Nor does he provide – and this is the crucial failing – any *analysis* of the way in which they affect mark-ups and hence relative shares.

Thus, we are left with a set of unanswered questions. Are the overhead and net profit components of gross non-wage income related? If so, do they move in the same or in opposite directions? Over what time-scale, and why? How does *international* competition affect the degree of monopoly in any individual country? (In dealing with k, Kalecki makes the implicit and very questionable assumption of a closed economy.) Are j and k wholly independent of each other, or would a sharp rise (fall) in j lead to a reduction (increase) in k to maintain the profit share, or the profit rate, at a constant level?

Without answers to these questions, we must conclude that Kalecki's account of relative shares tells us very little. His own empirical work, moreover, simply *measures* W/Y, j and k, and cannot be seen as providing empirical verification for *any* theory of relative shares. Kalecki's assumptions (constant ACV and SMC, mark-up pricing) are entirely realistic, but without an analysis of the determinants of the degree of monopoly his model yields no unambiguous predictions.[1]

Nevertheless, a generalised 'monopoly power' hypothesis remains intuitively appealing, and can be examined in a less formal and more subjective way. Okhawa [71], for example, links the sharp rise in the EC share in Japan immediately after 1945 with the dissolution of the Zaibatsu (although suggesting that the revival of trade unionism must also have played some part). Phelps Brown [9] found, for the United Kingdom in the nineteenth century, a tendency for distribution to swing in favour of labour when a 'hard' (highly competitive) market environment enforced upon firms an unusual degree of price restraint. It is not, however, clear that declining monopoly power can account for the near-universal increase in the labour share between 1914 and the 1920s, nor, unless intensified *international* competition is invoked, the recent profits squeeze.

Our tentative conclusion is that market imperfection is no more satisfactory as an explanation of changes in factor shares than the neo-classical theories of market perfection. Two further hypotheses remain (elements of both of which are also found in Kalecki's work). Distribution may depend on the outcome of conflict in the labour market; we discuss the impact of trade unions in Chapter 7. Or it may be influenced so overwhelmingly by macroeconomic forces as to render irrelevant reference to *any* particular micro market whatsoever. To this possibility we now turn.

[1] Moroney and Allen [65] found no significant correlation at the micro level between industrial concentration and the wage share. This is surprising, but it is *not* a refutation of Kalecki, since higher concentration may be offset by other (unspecified) factors. Nor is their avowedly 'neo-classical' explanation of variations in the wage share necessarily inconsistent with Kalecki's model.

6 Neo-Keynesian Theories

There is no single macroeconomic, or neo-Keynesian, theory of relative shares. Some models apply to the short run, others to the long run. Some assume the maintenance of full employment, others do not. One common strand, however, runs through them all: the treatment of 'entrepreneurial incomes as being the result of [the capitalists'] expenditure decisions, rather than the other way round – which is perhaps the most important difference between "Keynesian" and "pre-Keynesian" habits of thought' ([41] p. 94, n. 1).

This fundamental Keynesian insight may be built into a theory of relative shares in the following manner. Assume that a full employment equilibrium prevails. Now suppose that capitalists decide to invest a larger proportion of the given real income than was previously the case. Planned investment will now exceed planned savings. If equilibrium is to be restored, there must be an increase in the proportion of income which is saved. It is reasonable to suppose that capitalists have a higher propensity to save than do workers. Thus, the overall *ex ante* savings ratio may rise through an increase in the profit share in income at the expense of the pay share. If we ignore taxation and the possibility of borrowing abroad, then such a shift in relative shares is the *only* way in which the required increase in savings can be achieved.

This shift in relative shares is brought about by an increase in the price level. Since we have assumed full employment to prevail, an increase in investment expenditure cannot raise the level of real income. But *money* income will increase, in the same proportion as the price level. If money wages are unchanged,[1] real wages and the wage share will fall, while both money and real profits and the profits share will increase. By

---

[1] This assumption is of crucial importance; see below, p. 69.

57

deciding to spend more, the capitalists will have increased both their real incomes and their income share.

Kaldor's [41] is the best-known, though by no means the earliest, formulation of this argument. In his model investment is exogenously determined (at $\bar{I}$) by the state of confidence (or 'animal spirits') of the capitalists. Thus,

$$I = \bar{I}. \tag{21}$$

In equilibrium, planned investment equals planned saving, so that

$$I = S. \tag{22}$$

Workers save a constant (and possibly zero) proportion of their wages, s_w, and capitalists save a constant proportion of their profits (s_c, greater than s_w). Hence,

$$S = s_w W + s_c P, \qquad 0 \leqslant s_w < s_c < 1. \tag{23}$$

Finally, since wages and profits exhaust aggregate income,

$$W \equiv \Upsilon - P. \tag{24}$$

Substituting equations (22), (23) and (24) into (21), dividing both sides of the resulting equation by Υ, and rearranging terms, we derive the equilibrium profit share:

$$\frac{P}{\Upsilon} = \frac{\bar{I}}{\Upsilon} \frac{1}{s_c - s_w} - \frac{s_w}{s_c - s_w}. \tag{25}$$

Given the savings propensities of the two classes, the profit share depends solely on the ratio of investment to income, $\bar{I}/\Upsilon$, which is decided upon by the capitalists. An increase in the ratio of investment to income raises the share of profits through the inflationary mechanism described in the previous paragraph.

Fig. 2, which illustrates Kaldor's argument, is due to Atsumi [3] and Dodo [20]. Real income is fixed at the full employment level, Υ_f, so that

$$\Upsilon = \Upsilon_f. \tag{26}$$

Substituting (26) into (24), we have

$$P = \Upsilon_f - W, \tag{27}$$

which is the equation of the $\Upsilon_f \Upsilon_f$ line. This shows the various ways in which real income may be distributed between pay and profits. Its slope equals minus unity. From equations (21)–(23),

$$P = \frac{\bar{I}}{s_c} - \frac{s_w}{s_c} W. \tag{28}$$

Equation (28) gives the SS line. This shows the level of real profits which, for each level of real pay, will yield planned

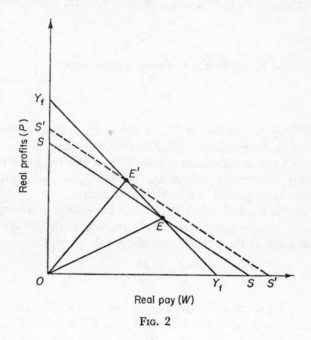

Real profits (P)

Real pay (W)

FIG. 2

savings exactly equal to $\bar{I}$. Its slope ($= -s_w/s_c$) is less than that of $\Upsilon_f \Upsilon_f$, since $s_w < s_c$. At E, income is distributed in such a way that planned savings equal planned investment at the full employment level of real income.[1]

The ratio of profits to pay, $P/W = (P/\Upsilon)/(W/\Upsilon)$, is shown by

[1] A single unique equilibrium is guaranteed only if s_w and s_c are constant with respect to W and P. If each class saves an increasing proportion of its income as that income increases, the SS curve may be concave rather than linear, and there may be *two* equilibria [3].

the slope of the ray OE from the origin. This allows us to trace out the distributive effects of a change in $\bar{I}$. If real investment increases, the SS curve will shift upwards to $S'S'$, which is parallel to SS, since s_w and s_c are unchanged. The new equilibrium distribution of income is established at E', where the share of profits is higher, and the share of pay lower, than before (the slope of OE' is greater than the slope of OE).

The model may be simplified by assuming that workers save nothing at all, so that $s_w = 0$. Equation (25) then becomes

$$\frac{P}{Y} = \frac{\bar{I}}{Y} \cdot \frac{1}{s_c}. \tag{25a}$$

In this case the SS line is horizontal, since now

$$P = \frac{\bar{I}}{s_c}, \tag{28a}$$

which is not a function of W. In the extreme case where it is also true that capitalists save *all* their income, and 'live on air', $s_c = 1$ and the profits share equals $\bar{I}/Y$. In this 'widow's cruse' case any increase in investment spending by the capitalists increases their profits *by exactly the same amount*.

It is now a simple matter to recast the model in a long-run form. In steady-state equilibrium growth, both income and capital grow at the natural rate of growth, g_n, so that

$$\frac{\Delta Y}{Y} = \frac{\Delta K}{K} = g_n. \tag{29}$$

But ΔK, the increase in the capital stock, is simply net investment, I.[1] Thus, $g_n = I/K = I/Y \times Y/K$, and $I/Y = g_n \times K/Y$, so that

$$\frac{P}{Y} = \frac{g_n v}{s_c}, \tag{30}$$

where $v \ (= K/Y)$ is the average *ex ante* capital output ratio. Moreover,

$$r = \frac{P}{K} = \frac{P}{Y} \cdot \frac{Y}{K} = \frac{P}{Y} \cdot \frac{1}{v} = \frac{g_n}{s_c}. \tag{31}$$

[1] Kaldor ([42] p. 312) defines investment and saving as *gross* of depreciation; but if this is done, equations (30) and (31) are no longer valid.

Equation (31) shows that the rate of profit depends solely on the natural rate of growth, g_n, and the capitalists' savings propensity, s_c. Marginal productivity plays no part in determining the rate of profit, and only a very limited role in the determination of the profits share (through its possible effect on v – see see [41] p. 98). It is no accident that Kaldor has become an increasingly vigorous critic of neo-classical theory as a whole (see especially [42]; also Pasinetti [73] ch. 6).

The simplicity of equations (30) and (31) appears to depend on the assumption that workers' savings are zero. If $s_w > 0$, in fact, there is a logical slip in Kaldor's analysis. If workers save, they acquire wealth, which – assuming that they receive a positive rate of interest on their savings – yields them property income. Equation (24) must then be replaced by

$$W \equiv \Upsilon - P_w - P_c, \tag{32}$$

where P_w and P_c are, respectively, workers' and capitalists' property incomes. Shares by income source now diverge from class shares, since the *workers'* share $(W + P_w)/\Upsilon$, is greater than the *employment income* share, W/Υ. What is more, Kaldor's equation (25) is invalid since it rests on the mutually inconsistent assumptions that $s_w > 0$ *and* $P_w = 0$.

Pasinetti was the first to notice this slip, and provoked a ferocious debate by demonstrating, in an article first published in 1962, that equations (30) and (31) are valid *even if* $s_w > 0$ ([72], reprinted in [73]). Pasinetti's proof rests on two assumptions. The first is that capitalists and workers receive the same rate of return on their savings; but this is not crucial. The second assumption, which *is* crucial, is a necessary condition for steady-state growth: the wealth of both classes must grow at the same rate, so that workers' and capitalists' shares of aggregate wealth remain constant. Given these assumptions, the proof is quite simple.[1]

[1] Let K_c be capitalists' property, and S_c their net savings. Then the first assumption implies that

$$P_c/K_c = P/K \ (= r).$$

The second assumption gives

$$S_c/K_c = S/K = I/K.$$

The neo-classical counter-attack aimed to restore the relevance of marginal productivity, which both Kaldor and Pasinetti had denied. It was spearheaded by Meade [64], and Samuelson-Modigliani [84]. However, their criticism is valid only if workers' assets increase more rapidly than those of the capitalists, whose total wealth declines towards zero. The *neo-classical* steady-state is thus one in which a 'bloodless revolution' [34] has vested ownership of all property in the hands of the workers, and eliminated the capitalists as a class. To put it mildly, this does not seem very plausible.

Pasinetti concludes that P/Y, W/Y and P/K depend only on the savings propensity of the capitalists, and are unaffected by changes in s_w. In principle this is *not* true of the *class* shares, P_c/Y and $(W+P_w)/Y$. But in practice the rate of return on workers' property is so low that P_w may be treated as negligibly small, even if s_w is in fact significantly greater than zero (see above, pp. 11, 12). Thus, neither the workers' share nor the share of employment income can be appreciably affected by a change in s_w.

Both [41] and [73] deal only with full employment equilibria. Their analysis is best interpreted as establishing that the achievement of full employment depends (given s_c and I/Y) on the achievement of the distribution of income given by equation (29) (see [73] pp. 118–20). If for some reason P/Y is greater than $(I/Y)/(1/s_c)$, full employment will prove unattainable, since savings will equal investment *too soon*, i.e. at a level of income below that required to sustain full employment. Analogous conditions for the achievement of full employment in the long run may be derived from equation (30).

This suggests that the basic neo-Keynesian model might be extended, in a more truly 'Keynesian' manner, to determine the *level* of income as well as its distribution. This might be done in two ways. The first introduces elements of neo-classical

---

Thus, $K_c = S_c \times K/I$ and

$$\frac{P}{K} = \frac{P_c}{K_c} = \frac{P_c}{S_c K/I} = \frac{IP_c}{S_c K} = \frac{I}{K} \cdot \frac{P_c}{s_c P_c} = \frac{1}{s_c} \cdot \frac{I}{K} = \frac{gn}{s_c}.$$

This gives equation (31); (30) may be derived by simple substitution.

theory which were clearly present in Keynes's own work. If the standard marginal equalities apply, the labour share equals the elasticity of output with respect to labour input, e_L. The property share equals the elasticity of output with respect to capital, which, with constant returns to scale, equals $(1 - e_L)$. Thus,

$$\frac{P}{W} = \frac{P/Y}{W/Y} = \frac{1 - e_L}{e_L}. \tag{33}$$

With a 'well-behaved' aggregate production function, this has the shape of OP^* in Fig. 3 [20]. The SS curve is that of Fig. 2,[1]

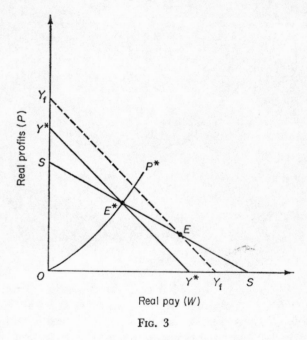

Fig. 3

and equilibrium is established at E^*, where OP^* intersects SS. Here, the distribution of income, given by equation (33), is such that aggregate savings equal aggregate investment. The

[1] For ease of comparison with Fig. 2, Figs 3 and 4 ignore the simplification allowed by Pasinetti's work (see above, pp. 60, 61). Our argument would be unaffected, however, if SS were derived – as a horizontal line – from equation (25a) instead of from (25).

equilibrium level of income is shown by Y^*Y^*, which is parallel to Y_fY_f but below it since, given the distribution of income and the savings propensities, investment is inadequate to sustain full employment.

Keynes might have been happy with Fig. 3. Kaldor would almost certainly prefer the alternative illustrated in Fig. 4.

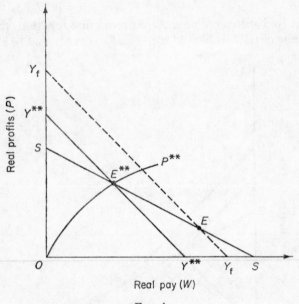

FIG. 4

Here OP^{**} reflects our old friend, the degree of monopoly.[1] Equilibrium is established at E^{**}, which is to be interpreted similarly to E^* in Fig. 3 except that it is excessive monopoly power, rather than the operation of pure competition, which makes profits (and hence savings) too large for Y_f to be achieved. In both cases something more than the neo-Keynesian equations (27) and (28) is required to give a determinate solution.

[1] Ignoring raw material costs, equation (20) in Chapter 5 may be simplified to $Y = (1+k)\ W$, so that $P/W = k$. The concavity of OP^{**} reflects Kalecki's belief that the degree of monopoly decreases as the level of economic activity increases.

And in both cases $\bar{I}/\Upsilon$ and s_c determine the *levels* of P and W rather than their relative shares.

All this rests on the assumption that only *one* commodity is produced. At the very least, however, we ought to distinguish between investment goods and capital goods, and to say something about relative shares in each of these two broad sectors. This gap is neo-Keynesian analysis has been enthusiastically filled by neo-classical economists. Solow's [90] is a two-sector variant in which sectoral shares depend on marginal productivity, but s_c determines the relative sizes of the investment- and consumer-goods sectors, and thus the weights to be applied to the sectoral shares in arriving at aggregate relative shares. Ferguson ([25] pp. 317–22) reaches the same destination by a more devious route. In both cases, however, the 'Keynesian' elements are merely the icing on what is essentially a neo-classical cake, a cake which is unpalatable for the reasons adduced in Chapters 3 and 4. Nor can composite models such as these be easily applied to empirical problems. If we are to adhere to our intention of confronting theory with evidence, it is the basic one-sector, full-employment neo-Keynesian model which must be assessed.

Empirical scrutiny of neo-Keynesian theory presents considerable difficulties. In its long-run form, the theory relates to conditions of 'golden age' steady-state equilibrium growth, which can rarely (if ever) have been experienced by capitalist economies. In the short run the position is less difficult, for equation (25a) can be applied to any situation in which full-employment equilibrium applies. It predicts that a change in the exogenous variable $\bar{I}/\Upsilon$ will cause the endogenous variable P/Υ to change in the same direction, and that this distributive shift will be greater, the smaller is the parameter s_c. There has been no rigorous empirical testing of this hypothesis.[1] In its absence, our assessment of the explanatory power of the neo-Keynesian theory must necessarily be highly tentative.

It must be noted, first, that many important changes in income distribution cannot be explained in this way. Variations

[1] An honourable exception is Reder's [76] early (1959) paper. But this attempts to test equation (25) rather than equation (25a) and must therefore he reckoned as unavoidably abortive.

in relative shares over the trade cycle, at least prior to 1939, are a case in point, since full employment was a feature only of a brief period in the upswing of each cycle. Similar difficulties arise with respect to long-run trends. The increase in the labour share in the United States, for example, appears to have occurred mainly in the 1930s, which were years of deep depression (see above, p. 21). For Britain, we know that the labour share was higher in 1921–4 (years of heavy unemployment) than in 1910–14 (when unemployment was quite low); and higher again in 1946–9 (with full employment) than in 1935–8 (with very high unemployment). Neo-Keynesian theory is able to say very little about such major distributive changes as these.

The period since 1945 and until quite recently, however, has seen something close to sustained full employment. The ratios of gross domestic fixed investment to gross national product, and of net domestic fixed investment to net national product, are shown in Fig. 5 for the United Kingdom between 1952 and

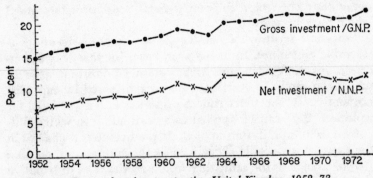

FIG. 5   *Gross and net investment ratios, United Kingdom, 1952–73*

1973. Both series fluctuate pro-cyclically, so that – if one is prepared to accept that post-war recessions did not represent significant lapses from full employment – a neo-Keynesian explanation for cyclical variations in relative shares does receive some support.

But both series also reveal a clear upward trend, the gross investment ratio rising from an average 15·8 per cent in 1952–4 to an average 21·2 per cent in 1969–73, and the net investment ratio from 7·5 to 11·9 per cent over the same period.[1] Thus neo-Keynesian theory predicts a declining labour share over the twenty years as a whole, which has most certainly not occurred. Nor, it appears, does the theory provide an acceptable explanation of the recent profits squeeze. While the gross investment ratio levelled off after about 1967, and the net investment ratio fell appreciably, both were consistently higher in the late 1960s and early 1970s than at any time in the 1950s, when the labour share was of course lower.

All in all, neo-Keynesian theory is no more successful in explaining movements in relative shares than the micro-economic models discussed in Chapters 3 and 5. It can be applied only to periods of full employment, and does not perform well even then. Clearly the capitalists' savings ratio s_c is *not* constant even in the short run. We shall consider the determinants of s_c in the course of the next chapter.

[1] It follows that this period does *not* represent an era of 'golden age' steady-state growth.

7 Unions and Relative Shares

The first point to be made is that the existence of a significant trade union influence on relative shares is consistent with *any* of the theories of income distribution outlined in the previous chapters. Consider first the neo-classical theory, in its popular, aggregate production function version. Union pressure might result in an increase in the real wage relatively to the rate of profit, that is, in an increase in w/r. The extent and direction of the effect of such an increase on relative shares depends entirely upon the elasticity of substitution between capital and labour (see above, pp. 32–5). If, as in the case of the Cobb–Douglas, $\sigma = 1$, relative shares will remain unchanged whatever happens to the ratio of input prices. If $\sigma > 1$, union pressure will have the (presumably unintended) effect of *reducing* labour's share. Only if $\sigma < 1$ will the labour share increase, and the property share decline. But some empirical studies of the aggregate production function (for what they are worth: see pp. 39–49) show an elasticity of substitution lower than unity. Neo-classical theorists must thus concede the possibility that unions might shift relative shares in favour of labour.

Rather stronger conclusions may be drawn if market imperfections are present. In a monopsonistic labour market, for example, the wage rate will be below the marginal revenue product of labour, and the firm will make excess (monopsonistic) profits. In restoring equality between wage and marginal revenue product, a union could redistribute these excess profits from the firm to its members. Similarly, the union might be able to transfer to its members part of the excess (monopolistic) profits of a firm operating in an imperfectly competitive product market. Both cases are examined, in partial equilibrium terms, by Bronfenbrenner [6]; Johnson and Mieszkowski [40], however, question their validity in a general equilibrium context.

Kalecki, it will be recalled, rejected marginalist theories of pricing outside pure competition. He suggested that unions might be able to limit the size of the mark-up applied by the firm to its average variable costs in pricing in imperfect markets, and in so doing increase the wage share at the expense of profits. We argued earlier (pp. 55, 56) that Kalecki's account of the determinants of the mark-up is unsatisfactorily vague, and similar criticisms may be made of his treatment [47] of the influence of trade unions. But the existence of some such influence, even if it cannot precisely be specified, is certainly consistent with the spirit of his argument, and suggests itself as an interesting research topic which has yet to be fully explored.

We saw also, in Chapter 6, that, contrary to Kaldor's assumption, the capitalists' savings propensity, s_c, has been subject to change even over quite brief periods. Rothschild offers one possible explanation for this variability in s_c, in terms of a 'reluctance of workers and trade unions to accept a deterioration of their acquired income in the face of rising investment' ([81] p. 656). This reluctance, reflected in militant wage bargaining, may set an upper limit – sometimes termed the 'inflation barrier' – to the ratio of investment to income. Alternatively, it may lead to an increase in the capitalists' savings propensity, so that the new and higher level of I/Y is financed out of a *constant* profits share.

As an extension of this line of thought, consider the possibility that unions might take the offensive, rather than seeking merely to defend an existing labour share. If capitalists' consumption can be squeezed by inducing an increase in s_c, and if I/Y genuinely is exogenously given, then it is clear from equation (25) in Chapter 6 that P/Y must fall. Conversely, periods of union weakness may allow a reduction in s_c and (for given I/Y) a corresponding increase in the property share.

At the theoretical level, then, and irrespective of the type of theory which is chosen, some degree of trade union influence on relative shares is clearly possible. To move from this conclusion to an assessment of the evidence involves a considerable jump. There is in fact considerable evidence from labour economists that unions are able to exert an important influence on the wages received by their members. For the United States, census data permit the isolation of union membership from other variables relevant in determining an individual's earnings, such as age, sex, occupation, experience and human capital ownership. Ryscavage [82] reports *ceteris paribus* earnings differentials between union members and non-members of the order of 20–40 per cent, and cites other authors in support. British data are much less comprehensive, and permit work only at the industry level. Researchers have attempted to discover whether it is true that, *ceteris paribus*, industries in which the majority of the labour force are union members display significantly higher levels of earnings than poorly-organised industries. Pencavel [74] argues that this is the case, but receives no support from Hood and Rees [38].

These studies, in any case, are not conclusive. There is good reason to believe that the mere fact of an individual's union membership, or of a high union 'density'[1] in an industry, does not entail that the union(s) in question are in a strong bargaining position *vis-à-vis* employers. Nor, as Purdy and Zis [75] make clear, can it be assumed that *growing* strength of numbers necessarily reflects enhanced bargaining power. Union power, moreover, need not always fully be used; it may, either deliberately or inadvertently, be held in reserve.

There are additional and quite different reasons for doubting that these studies are well suited to our present purposes. We wish to know whether unions have proved capable of redistributing income, in aggregate, from property to labour. Failure to improve the position of union members relative to non-members, even if proven, need not imply failure to increase the labour share as a whole. Union wage gains may 'spill over' to unorganised workers, perhaps because employers of non-union labour wish to forestall union recruiting drives (see Rees and Schultz [77]).

Furthermore, evidence that unions *have* generated and sustained a significant earnings differential over non-union labour is fully consistent with the proposition that they have been

[1] Union 'density' is defined as union membership divided by the numbers employed in the relevant categories.

unable to reduce the income share of property. The 'incidence of collective bargaining', to use a term introduced by Bronfenbrenner, remains uncertain. The union's gains may be at the expense of unorganised labour if, for example, union gains make non-members' pay lower than it would otherwise have been. In this case the only distributive effect is a shift *within* the labour share in favour of union members. Johnson and Mieszkowski [40], using a two-sector neo-classical model, argue that this will generally be the case. Alternatively, if union wage pressure generates sufficient aggregate demand to restore full employment where it had been lacking, or if it encourages accelerated productivity growth, relative shares may be very largely unaffected in any way.

The general evidence about the impact of trade unions on wages, then, tells us virtually nothing about the relationship between unions and income distribution. There exist, for the United States, some microeconomic studies, like those of Kerr [50] and Simler [86], which show that the labour share has not grown more rapidly in industries where unions are numerically strong, or growing fastest, than in unorganised sectors. But this too is inconclusive. We have already seen that union 'density' is not a satisfactory index of union power, and that spillovers may transfer gains from unionised to non-union sectors.

Cross-sectional international comparisons are probably more relevant, since spillovers are less likely to be important internationally. Here, the evidence is mixed. Kuznets [56] has shown that the share of employee compensation is positively correlated with *per capita* real income. Since unions tend to be stronger in rich than in poor countries, it is tempting to conclude that differences in union power are responsible for this correlation. But the share of self-employment income is negatively correlated with income per head, so that there may be no correlation at all between union strength and the *labour* share (as defined above, p. 17). This conclusion is reinforced by Loftus [60], whose substantial international sample reveals only minor differences in the share of *employee compensation* in manufacturing between rich and poor countries.

If neither disaggregated studies nor international comparisons are especially helpful, perhaps something can be learned from national time-series data on aggregate shares. We saw, in Chapter 2, that in most advanced Western countries the labour share has shown an upward trend; and that for Britain and the United States there is evidence of a significant (non-cyclical) increase in the labour share over the last decade. It would be generally agreed, moreover, that the power of unions is higher now than a century ago; and that union militancy has been increasing (dramatically in Britain, perceptibly in the United States) in recent years. Is there after all a causal relationship between union power (however measured) and the labour share?

Consider first the long-run picture. In the United States any increase in the labour share before 1929 can hardly be attributed to the unions, whose influence was confined to a very small portion of the labour force. The explosive growth of union membership in the 1930s was certainly accompanied by an increase in the labour share, but it is very difficult to disentangle the effects of this from the impact of an exceptionally severe cyclical depression. Equally, the decline in the labour share in Nazi Germany, documented by Jeck [39], might have been due to the destruction of the unions. Or it might merely have reflected a combination of declining product market competition, increasing investment and the normal cyclical upswing in corporate profits.

In Britain the labour share was very much higher in 1921–4 than in 1910–14, while union strength had (on almost any measure) considerably increased. Phelps Brown [9] very plausibly interprets this substantial and permanent distributive shift as the product of militant defensive action by British unions in the post-war depression, coupled with the 'hard' market environment presented by intensified international competition.[1] The rapid and continuing growth of the Swedish unions, however, was accompanied by no secular increase in the labour share whatsoever. Clearly generalisation of any sort is very difficult.

It seems likely that union power has played some part in the recent 'profits squeeze', at least in Britain. Note that the

[1] But see [10], where Phelps Brown vigorously denies that British unions have ever had any major impact on relative shares.

increase in union militancy which is reflected in the 'wages explosion' of the 1970s is *not* chiefly responsible. Glyn and Sutcliffe [29] emphasise that the profits squeeze began (around 1964) *before* the upsurge in union militancy. The high level of union strength and militancy since 1945 may have been an important necessary condition for the squeeze, but the crucial precipitating factor, according to [29], has been the intensification of international competition since the early 1960s. It might well be expected that the profits squeeze itself would have been tightened since wages 'exploded' in 1969–70, and Tables 1 and 2 suggest that this is so. But, given the normal cyclical fluctuations in relative shares, it may be too early to give a conclusive answer to this question. In the case of the United States a note of caution must be sounded: Nordhaus's [69] explanation of the U.S. profits squeeze does not rely in any way on union power.

Two broad conclusions can be drawn from all this. The first is that a significant union influence on relative shares is consistent with *any* theoretical model of income distribution, from which it follows that evidence concerning the presence or absence of such influence cannot be used as a test to distinguish between the merits of the various theories. The second is that unions probably have had some influence, although the evidence is too weak, and the number of counter-examples too large, for union bargaining power to provide the *sole* explanation of the course of relative shares.

8 Conclusion

Readers who have endured this far will not be surprised to find that our conclusions are largely negative. There is very little evidence that relative shares are constant in the short or long run, but there is some support for the notion that labour's share has an increasing secular trend. None of the theories of relative shares performs very impressively. Neo-classical accounts of income distribution can be faulted on many grounds, of which reliance on the assumption of perfect competition is probably the most damaging. 'Degree of monopoly' explanations are inadequately specified, yielding few if any unambiguous predictions. In so far as neo-Keynesian theory can be formulated precisely, it turns out to be wrong. Finally, ignorance about the effects of trade unions on relative shares remains very substantial.

It would be comforting to believe that the problem itself is a trivial or meaningless one. Unfortunately, as we have argued in Chapter 1, this is not true either. Somewhat speculatively, we hazard the guess that it will not be solved without major advances in the theory of oligopoly, which is, after all, the predominant form of market structure throughout the capitalist world. At present the micro theory of oligopoly pricing is largely taxonomic, its macro implications largely unexplored, and the problem of relative shares, like the poor, is with us still.

Mathematical Appendix

A. THE FIRM: SOME IMPLICATIONS OF PROFIT MAXIMISATION

The relation between the firm's output, q, and its inputs of labour, L, and capital, K, is given by its production function

$$q = f(L, K), \tag{A1}$$

where $\partial q/\partial L$ and $\partial q/\partial K$ are the marginal physical products of labour and capital (MPP_L and MPP_K). The relation between output and price, p, is given by the demand curve:

$$p = g(q), \tag{A2}$$

and total revenue is

$$R = pq = qg(q). \tag{A3}$$

Marginal revenue (MR) is

$$MR = \frac{\mathrm{d}R}{\mathrm{d}q} = \left(p + q\frac{\mathrm{d}p}{\mathrm{d}q} \right). \tag{A4}$$

A necessary condition for profit maximisation is that the marginal cost of each input be equated to its marginal contribution to total revenue, i.e. to its marginal revenue product (MRP). We assume throughout that the firm is a pure competitor in its input markets, facing perfectly elastic input supply surves, so that the marginal cost of labour equals its price (the wage rate, w) and the marginal cost of capital equals its price (the rate of profit, r). Now the marginal revenue product of labour, MRP_L, is

$$
\begin{aligned}
MRP_L &= \frac{\partial R}{\partial L} = \frac{\partial}{\partial L}(pq) = \frac{\partial p}{\partial L}q + \frac{\partial q}{\partial L}p, \\
&= \frac{\mathrm{d}p}{\mathrm{d}q}\cdot\frac{\partial q}{\partial L}q + \frac{\partial q}{\partial L}p = \frac{\partial q}{\partial L}\left(p + q\frac{\mathrm{d}p}{\mathrm{d}q} \right), \\
&= MPP_L \times MR.
\end{aligned} \tag{A5}
$$

Similarly, $MRP_K = MPP_K \times MR$. Profit maximisation thus entails that

$$w = MRP_L = MPP_L \times MR \quad \text{and} \quad r = MRP_K = MPP_K \times MR.$$
$$\text{(A6)}$$

In the *special case* in which the firm is also a pure competitor in its *product* market, p is constant and $MR = p$. *In this case, MRP_L $= MPP_L \times p$*, which is the value of the marginal product of labour, VMP_L and similarly for capital. Thus equation (A6) becomes

$$w = VMP_L; \qquad r = VMP_K. \qquad \text{(A6a)}$$

Equation (A6a) is valid *only* in perfectly competitive product markets. In general, $MR < p$, so that $MRP_L < VMP_L$ and $MRP_K < VMP_K$.

B. THE ADDING-UP PROBLEM

Equation (A1) can be interpreted as an *aggregate* production function, where q, L and K are the aggregate quantities of (supposedly homogeneous) output, labour and capital; p is now the 'aggregate price of output'. Thus national income, Υ, is

$$\Upsilon \equiv pq. \qquad \text{(A7)}$$

If the aggregate production function is homogeneous of degree n, then it is true that

$$\lambda^n q = \text{f}(\lambda L, \lambda K), \qquad \text{(A8)}$$

so that, if both inputs change in the same proportion λ, output increases by the proportion λ^n. If $n > 1$ we have increasing returns to scale; if $n = 1$, constant returns to scale; and if $n < 1$, decreasing returns to scale.

The adding-up problem arose in the course of Wicksteed's [97] attempt to demonstrate the equivalence of Ricardo's residual rent with the imputation of a reward to land according to its marginal product. Given perfect competition in both input and output markets, and assuming constant returns to scale,

Wicksteed suggested that input rewards (imputed on the basis of marginal productivity) would sum to equality with the value of total output. Only if this could be demonstrated would marginal productivity theory be deemed a *consistent* theory of relative shares. Wicksteed's analysis was rather cumbersome. Flux [28] in a revision offered a greatly simplified version involving the use of Euler's theorem.

This theorem entails that, for homogeneous functions,

$$nq = \left(\frac{\partial q}{\partial L}L + \frac{\partial q}{\partial K}K \right) \tag{A9}$$

so that

$$pq \equiv Y = \frac{p}{n}\left(\frac{\partial q}{\partial L}L + \frac{\partial q}{\partial K}K \right). \tag{A10}$$

We may define the sum of relative shares (FS) as

$$\text{FS} \equiv wL + rK. \tag{A11}$$

In the special case where all product markets are perfectly competitive, we may substitute equation (A6a) into (A11) to obtain:

$$\text{FS} = LV \cdot MP_L + KV \cdot MP_K = p\left(\frac{\partial q}{\partial L}L + \frac{\partial q}{\partial K}K \right) \tag{A12}$$

so that, using (A10),

$$\text{FS} = nY, \quad \text{so that } \text{FS} \gtreqless Y \text{ as } n \gtreqless 1. \tag{A13}$$

With constant returns to scale, $n = 1$ and the adding-up problem is solved. With increasing returns to scale ($n > 1$), $\text{FS} > Y$, and vice versa.

In *long-run equilibrium* in perfect competition, the existence of constant returns to scale is *not* required to solve the adding-up problem. At the end of the last century, besides presenting a solution under constant returns to scale, Wicksell [96] demonstrated that, *in this case*, input rewards will add up to the value of total output even in the absence of constant returns to scale. Outside long-run equilibrium, even in perfect competition, this will *not* be so.

In general, product markets will not be perfectly competitive.

Thus we must substitute equation (A6) – not (6a)A – into (A11), obtaining

$$\text{FS} = MR\left(\frac{\partial q}{\partial L}L + \frac{\partial q}{\partial K}K\right) \tag{A14}$$

so that, from (A10)

$$\Upsilon = \left(\frac{p}{MR}\frac{1}{n}\right)\text{FS}. \tag{A15}$$

Now p/MR may be interpreted (see above, pp. 52, 53) as Kalecki's 'degree of monopoly', k, so that

$$\Upsilon = \frac{k}{n}\text{FS} \quad \text{and} \quad \Upsilon \gtreqless \text{FS as } \frac{k}{n} \gtreqless 1. \tag{A16}$$

In general, then, the adding-up problem is solved if and only if the aggregate production function is homogeneous of degree n, where $n = k > 1$.

C. THE ELASTICITY OF SUBSTITUTION

For a two-input production function of the type in (A1), elasticity of substitution can be written as

$$\sigma = \frac{\mathrm{d}(K/L)}{K/L} \bigg/ \frac{\mathrm{d}[(\partial Q/\partial L)/(\partial Q/\partial K)]}{(\partial Q/\partial L)/(\partial Q/\partial K)}. \tag{A17}$$

Given perfect competition, and assuming that input rewards are measured in terms of physical units of their own output,

$$\frac{\partial q}{\partial L} = w \quad \text{and} \frac{\partial q}{\partial K} = r. \tag{A18}$$

It follows that

$$\sigma = \frac{\mathrm{d}(K/L)}{K/L} \bigg/ \frac{(\mathrm{d}w/r)}{w/r}. \tag{A19}$$

Assuming that the production function is linear homogeneous, so that the adding-up problem is solved, relative shares can be expressed as functions of σ. Let

$$s = \frac{wL}{wL + rK} \qquad (A20)$$

be labour's share, and

$$z = \frac{s}{1-s} = \frac{L/K}{r/w}. \qquad (A21)$$

The effect of a change in K/L on labour's share can be written as

$$\frac{ds}{d(L/K)} = \frac{ds}{dz} \frac{dz}{d(L/K)}. \qquad (A22)$$

Evaluating (A22):

$$\frac{ds}{dz} = \frac{1}{dz/ds} = 1 \Big/ \frac{1}{(1-s)^2} = (1-s)^2,$$

$$\frac{dz}{d(L/K)} = -\frac{1}{r/w} \left[\frac{L/K}{(r/w)^2} \frac{d(r/w)}{d(L/K)} \right]$$

which can be written in terms of σ as

$$\frac{dz}{d(L/K)} = \frac{r}{w} \left(\frac{\sigma - 1}{\sigma} \right).$$

Hence,

$$\frac{ds}{d(L/K)} = (1-s)^2 \frac{r}{w} \left(\frac{\sigma - 1}{\sigma} \right);$$

hence $\qquad \dfrac{ds}{d(L/K)} = \;\; \lessgtr 0 \text{ as } \sigma \lessgtr 1.$ $\qquad (A23)$

Thus, an increase in the capital labour ratio, K/L, will increase labour's share if $\sigma < 1$; decrease it if $\sigma > 1$; and leave it unchanged if $\sigma = 1$. Bronfenbrenner [7], from whom this proof is derived, further shows that the *sensitivity* of relative shares to changes in relative input quantities also depends on σ. Similar results may be derived for changes in relative input prices.

Bibliography

[1] K. J. Arrow, H. B. Chenery, B. Minhas and R. M. Solow, 'Capital–Labour Substitution and Economic Efficiency', *Review of Economics and Statistics* (Aug 1961).

[2] A. B. Atkinson, *Unequal Shares: Wealth in Britain* (London: Allen Lane, 1972).

[3] H. Atsumi, 'Mr Kaldor's Theory of Income Distribution', *Review of Economic Studies* (1960).

[4] P. T. Bauer, 'A Note on Monopoly', *Economica* (May 1941).

[5] M. Bronfenbrenner, 'Neoclassical Macro-Distribution Theory', in [61].

[6] M. Bronfenbrenner, *Income Distribution Theory* (London: Macmillan, 1971).

[7] M. Bronfenbrenner, A Note on Relative Shares and the Elasticity of Substitution', *Journal of Political Economy* (June 1960).

[8] E. H. Phelps Brown, 'The Meaning of the Fitted Cobb–Douglas Production Function', *Quarterly Journal of Economics* (Nov 1957).

[9] E. H. Phelps Brown, 'The Long-run Movement of Real Wages', in *The Theory of Wage Determination*, ed. J. T. Dunlop (London: Macmillan, 1966).

[10] E. H. Phelps Brown, 'Minute of Evidence No. 38' to the Royal Commission on Trade Unions and Employers' Associations (London: H.M.S.O., 1967).

[11] E. H. Phelps Brown and M. Browne, *A Century of Pay* (London: Macmillan, 1968).

[12] E. H. Phelps Brown and P. Hart, 'The Share of Wages in National Income', *Economic Journal* (June 1952).

[13] E. Budd, 'Comment' on Goldberg, in [67].

81

[14] G. J. Burgess and A. J. Webb, 'The Profits of British Industry', *Lloyds Bank Review* (Apr 1974).

[15] E. H. Chamberlin, *The Theory of Monopolistic Competition*, 8th edn (Harvard University Press, 1962).

[16] D. G. Champernowne, 'Elasticity of Substitution: A Mathematical Note', *Economic Journal* (June 1935).

[17] J. B. Clark, *The Distribution of Wealth*, new edn (New York: Kelley, 1965).

[18] C. W. Cobb and P. H. Douglas, 'A Theory of Production', *American Economic Review* (Mar 1928).

[19] P. Davidson, *Theories of Aggregate Income Distribution* (Rutgers University Press, 1960).

[20] K. Dodo, 'A Study in Macro-Economic Theories of Distribution', *Kobe University Economic Review* (1965).

[21] P. H. Douglas, *The Theory of Wages* (New York: Macmillan, 1934).

[22] P. H. Douglas, 'Are There Laws of Production?', *American Economic Review* (Mar 1948).

[23] J. T. Dunlop, *Wage Determination Under Trade Unions* (Oxford: Blackwell, 1950).

[24] C. H. Feinstein, 'Changes in the Distribution of the National Income in the United Kingdom since 1860', in [61].

[25] C. E. Ferguson, *The Neoclassical Theory of Production and Distribution* (Cambridge University Press, 1969).

[26] F. M. Fisher, 'The Existence of Aggregate Production Functions', *Econometrica* (Oct 1969).

[27] F. M. Fisher, 'Aggregate Production Functions and the Explanation of Wages: A Simulation Experiment', *Review of Economics and Statistics* (Nov 1971).

[28] A. W. Flux, Review of [97], *Economic Journal* (June 1894).

[29] A. Glyn and R. Sutcliffe, *British Capitalism, Workers and the Profits Squeeze* (Harmondsworth: Penguin, 1972).

[30] S. A. Goldberg, 'Long Run Changes in the Distribution of Income by Factor Shares in Canada', in [67].

[31] A. Grant, 'Issues in Distribution Theory: The Measurement of Labour's Relative Share 1899–1929', *Review of Economics and Statistics* (Aug 1963).

[32] F. H. Hahn, *The Share of Wages in the National Income* (London: Weidenfeld, 1972).

[33] F. H. Hahn and R. C. O. Matthews, 'The Theory of Economic Growth: A Survey', *Economic Journal* (Dec 1964).

[34] G. C. Harcourt, *Some Cambridge Controversies in the Theory of Capital* (Cambridge University Press, 1972).

[35] K. Heidensohn, 'Labour's Share in National Income: A Constant?', *Manchester School* (Dec 1969).

[36] K. Heidensohn and J. J. Zygmant, 'On Some Common Fallacies in Interpreting Aggregate Pay Share Figures', *Zeitschrift für die Gesamte Staatswissenschaft* (Apr 1974).

[37] J. R. Hicks, *The Theory of Wages*, 2nd edn (London: Macmillan, 1963).

[38] W. Hood and R. D. Rees, 'Inter-Industry Wage Levels in U.K. Manufacturing', *Manchester School* (1974).

[39] A Jeck, 'The Trends on Income Distribution in West Germany', in [61].

[40] H. G. Johnson and P. Mieszkowski, 'The Effects of Unionisation on the Distribution of Income: A General Equilibrium Approach', *Quarterly Journal of Economics* (Nov 1970).

[41] N. Kaldor, 'Alternative Theories of Distribution', *Review of Economic Studies* (1955-6).

[42] N. Kaldor, 'Marginal Productivity and the Macro-Economic Theories of Distribution', *Review of Economic Studies* (1966).

[43] N. Kaldor, 'Some Fallacies in the Interpretation of Kaldor', *Review of Economic Studies* (1970).

[44] M. Kalecki, *Essays in the Theory of Economic Fluctuations* (London: Allen & Unwin, 1939).

[45] M. Kalecki, *The Theory of Economic Dynamics* (London: Allen & Unwin, 1954).

[46] M. Kalecki, *Selected Essays on the Dynamics of the Capitalist Economy* (Cambridge University Press, 1971).

[47] M. Kalecki, 'Class Struggle and the Distribution of National Income', *Kyklos* (1971).

[48] R. R. Keller, 'Factor Income Distribution in the U.S.

During the 1920s: A Re-examination of Facts and Theory', *Journal of Economic History* (Mar 1973).

[49] C. Kennedy and A. P. Thirlwall, 'Technical Progress: A Survey', *Economic Journal* (Mar 1972).

[50] C. Kerr, 'Labor's Income Share and the Labor Movement', in *New Concepts in Wage Determination*, ed. G. W. Taylor and F. C. Pierson (New York: McGraw-Hill, 1957).

[51] L. R. Klein and R. F. Kosubud, 'Some Econometrics of Growth: Great Ratios of Economics', *Quarterly Journal of Economics* (May 1961).

[52] I. Kravis, 'Relative Income Shares in Fact and Theory', *American Economic Review* (Dec 1959).

[53] I. Kravis, 'Income Distribution: Functional Shares', in *International Encyclopaedia of the Social Sciences*, ed. D. L. Sills (New York: Macmillan and Free Press, 1968) 7.

[54] E. Kuh, 'Income Distribution and Employment over the Business Cycle', in *The Brookings Quarterly Econometric Model of the US*, ed. J. Duesenberry *et al.* (Chicago: Rand McNally, 1965).

[55] P. Kumar, *Long Run Changes in the Labour Share of National Income in Canada 1926–1966* (Queens University Industrial Relations Centre, Kingston, Ontario, 1971).

[56] S. Kuznets, 'Quantitative Aspects of the Economic Growth of Nations: IV. Distribution of National Income by Factor Shares', *Economic Development and Cultural Change* (Apr 1959).

[57] S. Lebergott, 'Factor Shares in the Long Term: Some Theoretical and Statistical Aspects', in [67].

[58] J. Lecaillon, 'Changes in the Distribution of Income in the French Economy', in [61].

[59] A. H. Leigh, 'Von Thünen's Theory of Distribution and the Advent of Marginal Analysis', *Journal of Political Economy* (Dec 1946).

[60] P. J. Loftus, 'Labour's Share in Manufacturing', *Lloyds Bank Review* (Apr 1969).

[61] J. Marchal and B. Ducros (eds), *The Distribution of National Income* (London: Macmillan, 1968).

[62] A. L. Marty, 'Diminishing Returns and the Relative

Share of Labor', *Quarterly Journal of Economics* (Nov 1953).

[63] K. Marx, *Capital* (Moscow: Foreign Languages Publishing House, 1962) 3.

[64] J. E. Meade, 'The Outcome of the Pasinetti Process: A Note', *Economic Journal* (1966).

[65] J. R. Moroney and B. T. Allen, 'Monopoly Power and the Relative Share of Labour', *Industrial and Labor Relations Review* (Jan 1969).

[66] V. N. Murti and V. K. Sastry, 'Production Functions for Indian Industry', *Econometrica* (Apr 1957).

[67] National Bureau of Economic Research, 'The Behaviour of Income Shares', *Studies in Income and Wealth* (Princeton University Press, 1964) 27.

[68] *National Income and Expenditure 1963–1973* (London: H.M.S.O., 1974).

[69] W. D. Nordhaus, 'The Falling Share of Profits', *Brookings Papers on Economic Activity* (1974).

[70] W. Oi, 'Labor as a quasi-fixed factor', *Journal of Political Economy* (Dec 1962).

[71] K. Okhawa, 'Changes in National Income Distribution by Factor Share in Japan', in [61].

[72] L. L. Pasinetti, 'The Rate of Profit and Income Distribution in Relation to the Rate of Economic Growth', *Review of Economic Studies* (1962).

[73] L. L. Pasinetti, *Growth and Income Distribution: Essays in Economic Theory* (Cambridge University Press, 1974).

[74] J. Pencavel, 'Relative Wages and Trade Unions in the U.K.', *Economica* (May 1974).

[75] D. Purdy and G. Zis, 'Trade Unions and Wage Inflation in the U.K.: A Reappraisal', in *Inflation and Labour Markets*, ed. D. Laidler and D. Purdy (Manchester University Press, 1974).

[76] M. W. Reder, 'Alternative Theories of Labor's Share', in *The Allocation of Economic Resources: Essays in Honour of B. F. Haley*, ed. M. Abramowitz (Stanford University Press, 1959).

[77] A. Rees and G. P. Schultz, *Workers and Wages in an Urban Labor Market* (Chicago University Press, 1970).

[78] P. A. Riach, 'Kalecki's "Degree of Monopoly" Reconsidered', *Australian Economic Papers* (1971).

[79] J. Robinson, *The Economics of Imperfect Competition* 2nd, edn (Macmillan: London, 1969).

[80] W. W. Rostow, 'Mr. Kalecki on the Distribution of Income 1880–1913', Appendix to *British Economy of the Nineteenth Century* (Oxford: Clarendon Press, 1948).

[81] K. W. Rothschild, 'Themes and Variations: Remarks on the Kaldorian Distribution Formula', *Kyklos* (1965).

[82] R. M. Ryscavage, 'Measuring Union–Non-Union Earnings Differences', *Monthly Labor Review* (Dec 1974).

[83] E. D. A. St Cyr, 'Notes on the Behaviour of Profit Shares in British Manufacturing Industries', *Manchester School* (June 1972).

[84] P. A. Samuelson and F. Modigliani, 'The Pasinetti Paradox in Neoclassical and More General Models', *Review of Economic Studies* (Oct 1966).

[85] C. L. Schultze, 'Short Run Movements of Income Shares', in [67].

[86] N. J. Simler, 'Unionism and Labor's Share in Manufacturing Industries', *Review of Economics and Statistics* (Nov 1961).

[87] H. A. Simon and F. Levy, 'A Note on the Cobb–Douglas Function', *Review of Economic Studies* (June 1963).

[88] R. M. Solow, 'Technical Change and the Aggregate Production Function', *Review of Economics and Statistics* (Aug 1957).

[89] R. M. Solow, 'A Sceptical Note on the Constancy of Relative Shares', *American Economic Review* (Sep 1958).

[90] R. M. Solow, 'Distribution in the Long and the Short Run', in [61].

[91] G. J. Stigler, *Production and Distribution Theories* (New York: Macmillan, 1946).

[92] B. Thalberg, 'Stabilisation Policy and the Non-Linear Theory of the Trade Cycle', *Swedish Journal of Economics* (Sep 1971).

[93] A. P. Thirlwall, 'Changes in Industrial Composition in the U.K. and the U.S. and Labour's Share of National

Income 1948–1969', *Bulletin of the Oxford University Institute of Economics and Statistics* (Nov 1972).

[94] R. Titmuss, *Income, Distribution and Social Change* (London: Allen & Unwin, 1962).

[95] A. Walters, 'Production and Cost Functions: An Econometric Survey', *Econometrica* (Jan–Apr 1963).

[96] K. Wicksell, 'On the Problem of Distribution', and 'Marginal Productivity as the Basis of Distribution', both in *Selected Papers on Economic Theory* (London: Allen & Unwin, 1956).

[97] P. H. Wicksteed, *An Essay on the Co-ordination of the Laws of Distribution* (London: Macmillan, 1894).

[98] A. Woodfield, 'Biased Efficiency Growth and the Declining Relative Share of Labour in New Zealand Manufacturing', *Southern Economic Journal* (Jan 1973).